WHAT NOT TO SAY

A Practical Guide to Supporting Bereaved Parents

By: Kiki Deville

ISBN: 9798337708119

DEDICATION

This Book is dedicated to: *Christopher Robinson.*
The best Daddy Dexter and Arlo could ever have had.

Dexter. For making me the best version of myself.

THIS ISN'T A BOOK ABOUT DEATH.

It will talk about it a lot. It will be mentioned many times. Death is not the reason you are here. Caring, thoughtfulness and compassion are why you are here.

But the real reason you are here is love.

We are seldom taught the tools to deal with death, especially the death of a child. This book has been written to introduce you to some of the knowledge and tools needed to support a loved one through this difficult time. You can read it whichever way suits you, but it has been written to help you navigate from the start of the journey if that is where you find yourself. You can read it straight through or dip in and out, whatever feels most helpful.

There may be some repetition of actions you can do, but it is worth pointing out that you can do them in different scenarios. Most of these things will apply to other bereavements too, so use the information as you see fit.

At the end of each chapter, you will see my *Wisdom Nuggets*. These are the practical things that you can do and say to offer support. This is not an exhaustive list but has been compiled from many conversations over the years with parents who have survived through the toughest of situations.

Whether this is playing out now, or you have come into someone's life many years after the death of their child, the same advice applies. When you lose a child, it is a forever thing, so this isn't information just for the beginning. This is a guide for a lifetime.

In my real life, part of my job is to make people laugh. After my son Dexter died, I didn't think I would ever laugh again, but now comedy is a core part of how I navigate the world. A world that fundamentally changed the day I found out that I would outlive one of my children.

Therefore, there may be parts that you read here that are deliberately written to bring light, or specifically, to make you laugh. They are to bring levity to a dark subject but in no way are they to disrespect bereavement. We need balance, and these moments are purely my entertainer's way of bringing light in where I can.

When confronted with death, human nature will automatically see us meditate on how it has impacted our own lives. These conversations can stir the feelings that we may have repressed or felt we had reconciled, but the very nature of grief is that we can never predict how it will work, or when it will rear its ugly head. So, there may be elements of this book that make you revisit some of those hard and painful feelings you had when death showed its hand in your life. It is important that you look after yourself in those moments.

That said, and I say this with love, this is not about you.

Contents

INTRODUCTION

If you are here, it is most likely because someone you know, and possibly love, has experienced the unthinkable: the death of their child.

You are probably wondering what the right thing to say to them is, and how to find words that will bring comfort in the darkest of times. As someone in this club that nobody wants to join, and with the benefit and privilege of having worked with many bereaved families since my own child died in 2007 – I am here to help you find those words.

First things first, please don't feel bad for saying the "wrong" thing. This is not an exercise in shame, but rather a place to find compassionate and thoughtful words, and importantly, actions, of comfort. We have all said things that we then revisit in our head for the next 20 to 45 years at 3 am because we are mortified that we ever said anything so "stupid," but I firmly believe that in most situations, no one sets out to hurt anyone with insensitive comments. Honestly, for me, I'd rather someone said something misguided, than nothing at all!

For far too long, we have placed the burden of addressing how we talk about, and experience the death of a child, on bereaved families alone. As a society, we have prioritised our own fears and discomfort above the pain and heartache of people going through one of the worst losses a human being can experience. Mostly because it makes us uncomfortable. We don't want to think about it happening to us. I am not unsympathetic of course. It is horrible to think of something happening to your child. The idea of it is terrifying, but for most, it is just that, an idea. For those of us with this lived experience, it is a reality.

In the UK, comfort and politeness are often prioritised over honesty, even if that causes someone emotional harm. The truth is we are not owed comfort. It is not a right. Of course, it is nice when we are comfortable, but it should never be more important than someone's grief. I have often said that as an Australian I felt like I had the advantage that people just kind of expect me to be direct when talking about bereavement (or anything else for that matter!) so they're not surprised when I'm mouthy. (I prefer the word "challenging", but this is one instance where English people might not be so polite about it)!

Most people are generally wonderful at the beginning of a bereavement. Then life, of course, for everyone else, moves on, and we are left with our own thoughts and memories and a lifetime's worth of love with nowhere to put it. For some, we may become active in raising money and awareness for the terrible things that have robbed our children of their futures. For others, our focus may move entirely into forgetting as well as we can. There is simply no roadmap for how you get through the days, mostly alone, to try to live some semblance of a normal life again. It is impossible to say that there is a "correct" way to do this.

Within it, we are often reminded by others, without experience, of how they believe we should be doing. That is why I have written this all down. To empower you with tools to help the people you know, and want to help, with the benefit of my experience.

It is important to remind you that despite our best efforts to help you understand the ways you can support us, we are not always right, or even fair. A bereaved parent may not always hear things how they were intended, and we may take things the wrong way from time to time. We may also forget things that were said and done. You need to forgive us this as our life has just been taken apart in front of our very eyes, so we don't always see all the things as they happen. As a result of the trauma that arises from the death of a child, it is true that our brain's "editing software" may not be doing its full job, so this is why we need you to understand why what you say matters, including how you say it.

I need to explain how I arrived here, writing quite a niche book on helping bereaved parents. This is how my life changed beyond recognition and tore at the very fabric of everything I would ever know and love. It is also how I realised that my life needed to be dedicated to changing the way that we support, view and recognise bereaved parents.

Born and raised in Australia in the 1970s (let's say "mid" for my ego), at the beginning of 2003, I moved to America to pursue my career as a blues singer, a dream since childhood. As a singer, the US is where I thought I naturally needed to be and oh, how I loved it! It was the most amazing and transformative year of my life. I was divorced, single, loving life and committed to my career 100%. Then a northern Englishman walked into the hostel in West Hollywood where I lived and worked, and my life took a completely different turn.

On holiday to meet some friends returning from a gap year, Chris and two university friends turned up to my hostel and I immediately noticed his big blue eyes and shy smile. We hit it off at check-in, with me deciding I had been comedy gold for the last 20 minutes, and they invited me for a drink after my shift.

We had a beer and I asked what they all did for a living. Stuart, the dry, northern, diabetic whom we affectionately refer to as Sugar-Free Stu, said, "We work in computers." Chris, without missing a beat added "Well not IN computers, because it's small and there's fans and stuff." My guffaw at this made it pretty clear how things were going to go that night.

Hundreds of long-distance phone calls, MSN Messages (it was the early noughties after all), and emails, 5 months later, in January of 2004, I moved to the UK.

Chris and I married in the spring of 2005 and with me being 6 years older than him, we needed to think about trying for a baby if we were serious about having a family.

We got pregnant quickly but sadly, this turned out to be a partial molar pregnancy and I had a missed miscarriage.

A molar pregnancy[1] usually happens when two sperm fertilise a nor-

---

1   https://www.rcog.org.uk/for-the-public/browse-our-patient-information/mo-

mal egg meaning the developing foetus has three sets of chromosomes (rather than two); two from the father and one from the mother. Go Chris and your super sperm! They are rare and the pregnancy cannot survive. As I had a partial molar pregnancy, thankfully, I didn't have to have follow-up treatment of chemotherapy after an operation to remove all of the molar tissue, but I did have to pee in a cup for two years and send it to Sheffield to make sure nothing else developed. Oh, the glamour! I have no idea what they did with the pee. Who knows, perhaps out there is a clone of a fifty-something-year-old woman with no sense of direction and a penchant for shoes and the dramatic?

We got pregnant again within a few months and had a very early scan at the 8-week mark. When pregnancies don't go to plan, it is often within the 7–9-week timeframe, so providing there is a heartbeat at this early scan, it will usually be determined that things should be okay going forward.

After visiting Australia, we returned home at 22 weeks pregnant and went for our second scan. The radiographer showed us the heartbeat, but then immediately turned the screen around and clicked away, the tension palpable. By the time she stopped to face us, we knew something wasn't right. "Baby's heart is very strong, so that is an excellent sign," she said, but there was concern in her voice and we could see things were about to go horribly wrong. "I'm afraid that there are some concerns about Baby's measurements." Shock soon set in.

A 20-week scan has a very specific purpose. It is an anomaly scan, *not* a gender scan. Among other things, it is designed to check for about 11 conditions that would probably not have been detected by this stage of pregnancy. Conditions like Edwards or Patau's syndrome are detected at this stage, along with other conditions like spina bifida or cleft lip. Conditions like cleft lip, are not considered life-threatening or life-limiting, so a positive outcome can still be expected. Conditions like Edwards syndrome, however, are fatal in the first year in 90-95% of babies. When you have this kind of diagnosis, you are referred to genetic counselling and there are some big discussions and even bigger decisions to be

lar-pregnancy-and-gestational-trophoblastic-disease/

made. Surely we wouldn't have to do that? Surely everything would be okay?

We were told that we would need to go urgently to St Marys Hospital in Manchester to have an amniocentesis. This test is for chromosomal conditions like Down's syndrome but also tests for some genetic conditions like Turner syndrome. The drawback? It can't test for everything, and it carries a 1 in 100 risk of miscarriage. [2]

According to the test results, our baby (which we know now is a boy), does not have a chromosomal issue nor does he have any of the genetic conditions that this procedure tests for. In fact, in the opinion of the doctors, all the determining measurements are at the top end of normal and should "probably" make for a normal outcome. Our geneticist talked us through possible syndromes that aren't tested for.

The word "syndrome" in simple terms means a group of symptoms which consistently occur together and are associated with a particular condition. It can be anything from a learning difficulty to curly hair, but some conditions are, obviously, much worse than others. Some are survivable, some are not.

I should interject here by saying that this is not an indictment of the medical profession. There are simply too many conditions that a human being can have, some we can test for, many we cannot. According to geneticists, we all carry one to two gene mutations that can cause severe disorders or prenatal death. [3]

It is a lottery and not the kind I get excited about! No healthcare system can be expected to test for every possible outcome. That said, once conditions become more clearly prevalent or simple to test for, then there really is no excuse not to. We left the hospital that day knowing that our baby would be special, but little did we know how much.

Chris had been adamant that I should not go into labour at rush hour

2   https://www.nhs.uk/conditions/amniocentesis/risks/#:~:text=If%20you%20
have%20amniocentesis%20after,can%20lead%20to%20a%20miscarriage
3   https://www.sciencedaily.com/releases/2015/04/150408100522.htm#:~:text=Sum-
mary%3A,inherited%2C%20according%20to%20new%20estimates

as we had to drive to Manchester, and we were already almost an hour away. After an event-free remainder of the pregnancy, at 6.30 am on September 12, 2007, my waters broke. Rush Hour. We called the hospital and because of the distance, they suggested we come in. I was doing okay, and we had attended the birthing classes at the hospital weekly. We had a rough plan, but I was willing to use pain relief if I needed to (which meant I was definitely going to use pain relief). Things didn't move along and there was meconium in my waters which showed the baby was in distress, so we agreed to induction drugs.

My whole life I have had low blood pressure, and it turns out that doesn't go well with anaesthetics. Cue me fainting and the anaesthetist emphatically telling me that, no, I could not have any more epidural as they would like to keep my heart beating thanks very much. So, gas and air only for pain relief it was.

If you've ever been in labour and someone says you'll be fine with gas and air; they are lying. Childbirth hurts. (Clearly, some people find it easier. My friend Lisa barely felt either of her children!) Despite the pain, at just past 6 pm, Dexter William Robinson entered the world. Blue and silent.

I don't remember him being resuscitated. I only remember him being given to me and looking at his perfect little face and my heart whispering "Something is wrong." We were moved on to a ward with other new additions, but we had a sense that something wasn't quite right. Dexter wouldn't cry and didn't seem interested in feeding and he had no muscle tone at all.

Having returned from meeting their first grandchild, my niece, who had been born in Norway a few months earlier, my mother and father-in-law came to the hospital in the morning to meet their first grandson moments before he was whisked away to the special care baby unit upstairs. It had been a very long night of trying to get Dexter to feed, but he wasn't showing any signs of improvement by the morning.

When a baby goes into special care from the ward, it's done without the parents as it can be very distressing. Watching your baby have a cannula fitted is not what you are expecting at this point. Seeing your baby on that ward for the first time can be enormously overwhelming. There are tubes and wires and monitors and all coming out of this tiny baby. Dexter was full-term, so he wasn't super small compared to the preemies, but he still looked so little and so very vulnerable.

Within a short space of time, the geneticist had come to the ward to examine him. About 20 minutes later we were taken into a small room. Me, Chris, the ward sister, the geneticist and my mother and father-in-law.

"I believe he has Zellweger Syndrome. It is a genetic metabolic disorder."

Okay. What does that mean?

"He is going to die."

The shock was like a punch in the face. It was like someone else was controlling my body and I wasn't sure that my heart would continue to beat. The entire world was suddenly moving in slow motion, and I had to literally remind myself to breathe.

I asked what it meant, not really understanding that this lovely doctor had just told us our son was going to die. At no point did I expect the next words.

"In my experience of this disease, he will not survive longer than six months, but more than likely, it will only be a few months." How could he have something that meant he would die? But then also that he would die so soon.

Then, the most British thing in the world happened. At the very moment that my heart was breaking in two, a nurse burst into the room with four cups of tea. It was the start of about a billion cups of tea that would be prepared for us over the coming months. To this day I only drink tea if I'm really poorly. I just can't bear the taste of it.

We went in to see Dexter. As I write this, I can still feel him in my arms and the despair of not knowing if I would ever know happiness again. This perfectly formed, beautiful baby was going to leave us sometime very soon and there was absolutely nothing we could do about it. No amount of fight or fundraising would save him. We were devoid of the most basic human need, hope.

Zellweger syndrome is a peroxisomal biogenesis disorder. A very rare metabolic disorder that is on a spectrum confusingly known as Zellweger syndrome or the Zellweger spectrum disorder. On that spectrum, known at the time, there were four dominant conditions. All are serious but not all are fatal in infancy. Some are survivable into early childhood or even adolescence. Dexter had the most severe form. He would die within 12 months, but most probably much sooner.

Zellweger syndrome is an autosomal recessive inherited disorder. In other words, both Chris and I carry the defective gene. As do both of our parents and theirs and so on. We had a 1 in 4 chance that any baby we had would have the disease and a 1 in 2 chance that any child we had would also be a carrier. We had a 1 in 50 million chance that we would meet and carry this in the first place. In any other scenario, these kinds of chances would be amazing. In this one though, they were devastating.

After a week of learning how to take care of him, we had decided that we needed to be at home, so off we went with our special boy. The next day, the team from Derian House Children's Hospice came to visit us. We weren't interested in going there. We didn't want to see this place of death thanks very much but sure, come back next week if you want.

It's natural to dismiss hospice care. After all, we associate it with the palliative care of the elderly or cancer patients, not with children. I also wasn't ready to face the fact that he was going to die. Going to a hospice was going to make that pretty darn real!

Every day we set about doing things with him, trying to fill a lifetime of memories into whatever amount of time we would be lucky enough to get. Then every night when we sat down to dinner, just me, Chris, and Dexter in his Moses basket in between us, I would cry.

When your child is diagnosed with a life-limiting condition you start your journey with *anticipatory grief*. In other words, you begin to start the process of grieving. I would love to be able to tell you that it makes the acute grief when your child does die much easier, but it doesn't. It kind of starts all over again. It is a terribly lonely place to be as it is horribly misunderstood.

The weeks passed and at 4 weeks old, we had a 1-month birthday party for him. My sister-in-law came from Norway with our new niece, Dexter's cousin, who was just about 3 months old by then. Our friends and family surrounded us, and we celebrated our special little boy.

By this time though we were exhausted and somewhere in these weeks that blur into one, Derian House had managed to convince us to visit. Going up the driveway is one of the hardest journeys I have ever made, but inside the building couldn't have been further from what I had expected.

It turns out that Derian House is one of the most life-affirming places I have ever known. Somehow, it's sunny on the inside and it is full of the most incredible people who are called to do what they do. And oh, how they love a baby!

A few days after his birthday party we called Derian and asked if we could come in to stay. One of their superpowers is hearing desperation and somehow, they knew we needed to be there, so they found us space.

When you become a parent, you never imagine you will have to think of the way that you would like your child to die. Sure, every parent has that fear of the worst happening, it is human nature. But to have to think about and discuss how you want their final moments to be; is a whole other ball game. After much discussion, and an abundance of tears, we knew how we wanted it to be, now we had to hope that life/the universe/God/whatever, didn't have other plans.

The doctor at Derian House did tell us that night that Dexter wasn't doing well. His oxygen levels were very low, and he needed piped oxygen almost constantly, but still, we didn't really feel like it was going to happen yet. We agreed to gentle, non-invasive resuscitation with our nurse, and we went to get our bags to take upstairs to the family flat we would stay in overnight whilst Dexter was watched over by wonderfully experienced, caring staff.

When we returned to his room there was a flourish of activity and his tiny body lay on the bed in front of us. "I'm so sorry, but I couldn't bring him back."

I threw myself on him and screamed his name. Every part of me inside shattered. A darkness moved into my body that I thought I would never overcome. This wasn't what we'd planned. It was supposed to be peaceful; we were supposed to be with him. We never should have left him alone. I pleaded with him to breathe.

Without warning, he opened his eyes and took an enormous breath in. It was like he sucked all the oxygen from the room as me and Chris and the nurse held our collective breath and waited to see if he would continue to breathe. Miraculously, he did. My boy was back with me. He wasn't going to leave us just yet.

His little body was shutting down, but he had managed to come back and hold on for us to have these moments we had planned through sobs of despair. Through the anger that this was happening and through the guilt and shame I had for every bad decision I had ever made throughout my life, my overwhelming sense was this was all my fault. Many years later, and hours and hours of therapy have made me realise this just simply wasn't true.

Over the next hours, we laid down with him on the bed. Holding him between us, we stroked his face and told him all the plans we'd had and how we knew he would have been the smartest and kindest boy in the world. We would make sure everyone knew his name.

At just after 1 am on October 15, 2007, we laid his tiny body in the cot in his hospice room, kissed his beautiful face and said goodbye to our son forever.

When your child dies, the loneliness is profound. All the colour left my world and all I saw was darkness. I thought I would never see light or know joy or laughter again and I felt the most overwhelming sense of failure that I couldn't make my son healthy. He died and all the confidence drained from my very being.

I promised Dexter in his dying moments that I would make sure he changed the world. He had most definitely changed mine. I wanted him to know we would never forget him. He will always be important, and my job now is to keep his memory alive.

Now you are reading this, you are the reason he will change things. You are how we will change the narrative and you are going to be the reason that the person or people you help with this knowledge are going to feel supported, loved and cared for and less alone. For that, sincerely, I thank you.

I said in the beginning this wasn't a book about death.

This is a book about love.

PART ONE

WHAT WE NEED YOU TO KNOW

It's difficult to explain the loneliness that comes with the loss of a child. When you become a parent, you can feel like, to begin with, you have one major responsibility; to protect your child. It is built into our DNA. Then suddenly, someone tells you that the child you have been thinking of for the last 9 months, the hopes and dreams and wishes you had for the future

Doctor/Lawyer/Nobel Peace Prize winner (or all the above) that you were bringing into the world to make it a better place, are all but gone. For some reason, of all the babies born in the world today (about 385,000 per day)[4], *your* baby has been born with something wrong. Or of all the healthy children you know, *your* child has just been diagnosed with a life-limiting or life-threatening illness from which you have only hope and a prayer that they will recover from.

At this point, we are in survival mode. Someone is inevitably giving us endless cups of tea and we are scrambling to make sense of one of the most difficult conversations we have ever had. For some, we are being introduced to medical professionals who are going to teach us how to keep our child alive as long as possible. We may be having meetings with Paediatricians to decide on end-of-life care, and do we want a DNACPR (do not attempt cardiopulmonary resuscitation) or are we going to stay in the hospital or go home? We might be referred to a Children's Hospice, something we didn't even realise existed.

Or we may just be sat in a hospital room, holding this precious child trying desperately to understand how this could happen and wondering if we will ever, ever stop crying.

And then, all of a sudden, we realise something; we have to tell people.

---

4   https://www.theworldcounts.com/challenges/toxic-exposures/polluted-bodies/how-many-babies-are-born-a-day

Not only that, but we have to tell the people we love.

You might never have realised this, but telling the people we know and love that our child is going to die, is one of the toughest parts of all this. There are so many elements of it that are difficult, not least how upset we know you will be for us. We must live with the idea that we are shattering your innocence somehow. Many of us go through life not having to confront death without warning. We know it is inevitable, but we have the knowledge and understanding that eventually, life comes to an end. Sadly, we will be confronted by it in many ways through people we know, at times when we do not expect it, and times when we know it to be so horribly cruel. But even with that knowledge, the death of a child, or the expected death of a child, messes with everything we know to be natural, just and fair.

We know that in a small way, we are making parenthood, or the idea of parenthood that little bit more frightening for others. Something that billions of people do, can seem like a minefield of fear and hurt and can take away from some of the truly joyful parts of having children.

We also know that we are asking you to become a pivotal part of how we navigate through this next part of our lives, the "after." The pressure on you is real. Because, believe me, we will remember how you behaved. Bereaved parents will often discuss with each other the things people have done and said, and it never surprises me how vivid those memories are. Even for me, many years since Dexter's death, I remember things better than I remember what I went to the kitchen for! It doesn't mean we don't understand where these things might have come from, but we need you to remember that they stick.

It is important to know that we don't need you to fix anything. We don't need you to "know." We just need you to place yourself outside of this for the moment and be there for us in ways you may not understand or even agree with. We need you to be near, literally and metaphorically. Please acknowledge our child's existence and try to understand why our lives are so fundamentally changed. We don't want you to know. We don't want anyone to know.

A NOTE ON LANGAUGE

Many parents will refer to their child's death in different ways and none of those are necessarily right or wrong but rather, individual.

I have used the terms child death, child loss or losing a child throughout this book. Many bereaved parents do not like the phrase "lost a child" as they feel it implies some sort of lack on their part.

As it is a widely accepted phrase, I have continued to use it but would encourage you to listen closely to the language that parents are using and try to fall in line with that.

CHAPTER ONE

Apples And Oranges; Why Comparison Sucks

"Comparison is the thief of joy."

Theodore Roosevelt.

Death is not a competition.

When your child dies, in those first few days of barely being able to put one foot in front of the other, I can say with a great degree of certainty what most parents won't be thinking; "This would be so much harder if my child wasn't just a baby," or "I bet this would be easier if I had another child."

Variables like your child's age may be something we think about later, but I know for me, it took one conversation with another bereaved parent to truly understand why comparing our losses is not at all helpful.

I was fortunate enough to be a part of a bereavement group at Derian House called Stepping Stones. Each person in the group had lost their child around the same time as Dexter died - roughly around 6 months before the start of the group.

It is standard practice to start counselling in the hospice world after the six-month mark. Before this point, generally, parents are still in a very acute phase of grief. They are simply trying to imagine a world where their heart has not just been shattered into a million pieces.

I once spoke to a family who had a daughter who had died at 10 years old. I mentioned to her mum that I thought it must be so much harder for her because she knew her daughter's personality and they had memories of her growing and she had time with her. She knew her. She looked at me and gently said "Yes, I knew her, and I have memories of her growing and I had time with her. You never had any of that."

For people who have never had a child die, the idea that there is a difference between the death of a baby versus the death of a teenager seems like a reasonable comparison. Simply, it's not. This is nuanced of course, but ultimately, we are in the same place; that of being the parent of a child who has died.

The death of a child is not just about the physical demise.

The death of a child is the loss of all the hopes and dreams and wishes you had for that child. When these things begin may be different for people, but once your child is born, you will almost always have thoughts of all the future ahead for that tiny babe in arms. You will have imagined their smile and laugh, and you will have pondered who they will look like the most (secretly hoping it's you and not your Great Aunt Lorraine who rocked a moustache from the age of 3!) Will they be quiet like their dad? Or a show pony like their mother? (rude) Will they be sporty or academic? Of course, they will be both in your mind! When will they walk/talk/get their first tooth? All these things are normal parental feelings.

When your child dies, you are robbed of that future. And not just your child's future, but a future in which you are the same person as before. Arguably parenthood changes you anyway, but the death of a child can change you beyond recognition.

Through the work I have done with bereaved families, the most resounding thing I have seen is the evidence of undiagnosed post-traumatic stress disorder. It was at least 10 years before I realised that I was suffering from it myself. Like most people, I thought of PTSD as a wartime illness, something that came from combat. I didn't think of it as something that people in the regular world could even have.

Losing a child is ALWAYS traumatic. It doesn't matter if it was labelled a "traumatic" death. A child dying disrupts the natural flow of things, and therefore it has the capacity to change our brain mechanics. Trauma profoundly affects the brain. This is a known fact. [5]

To begin with, it shrinks the prefrontal cortex, the part of the brain that helps regulate mood and emotion and is also in charge of rational thought. This can be a big reason why we may move from hopeless to hysterical within moments. This part also oversees decision-making, which can feel more difficult at a time when so many complex things need to be done and big decisions need to be made.

It also shrinks the hippocampus, the area of the brain responsible for helping us differentiate between the past and the present. This part decides which memories will move from short-term to long-term memories, which is why we may not remember something that was said or done at the beginning of this grief.

Finally, our amygdala becomes overactive because of trauma, and this is the part of the brain that decides how we respond to stress. We may find it hard to calm down or can be hypersensitive to danger because of this.

I find it quite useful to remember that many of the elements of grieving like this, are determined by science. I think it can help to explain some of our behaviours and decisions to the people around us.

Trauma and grief may have quieter days, but they never leave us. One of the key things to remember about the loss of a future for us is that it is - in its very nature - ongoing. It is not just the first year. It is all the "firsts" after that.

It is the birthdays, the first days of school and so on. These are the "firsts' we will never have.

When I was pregnant with Dexter, it was at that point in my life when everyone I knew was pregnant. My sister-in-law, my best friend, my cousin. The list felt endless. Despite having some concerns during my pregnancy, I still enjoyed having this experience with the people closest to me. Dexter's death had an enormous impact on all these people, not least my sister-in-law. With just one exception, all the other pregnancies I knew of resulted in babies with no major health issues. In the July of

5   https://www.ptsduk.org/what-is-ptsd/the-science-and-biology-of-ptsd/

2007, we were blessed with a beautiful half-Scandinavian blonde bomb-shell of a niece, just a few months before Dexter was born.

I love my niece with all my heart (and her sister, who would be ever so annoyed should I not mention her!) but one thing never changes. She is a stark reminder of what I don't have. Obviously, that is not her fault, but it doesn't change the fact. It also makes her even more important to me.

My sister-in-law is just about the best person I could ever have been lucky to have in my life because she knows this. She is the person I can rely on the most to "get it right." She always acknowledges Dexter, and she always makes sure he has a presence in our family when we are together, lighting a candle or squeezing my arm to make sure I know she is aware. She has listened and acted in ways that have reduced me to tears because of her unconditional kindness. She has been patient with me and worried about me, and she has always been there advocating for her nephew of whom she was also robbed.

It is difficult in the throes of your grief to understand its impact on the people around you. She had just become a mother for the first time. She had moved to Norway after University, where she met her now Norwe-gian husband, and was living in a foreign country when my niece was born. Of course, my mother-in-law was there for her, but in essence, she was doing it away from home, a young woman navigating a roller coast-er of emotion, without nearly enough sleep, in a country and a language not her own. That is a tough place to be. Then her nephew was born, and she was told he was going to die.

My sister-in-law and my husband are incredibly close. There are only 18 months between them, and they spent their childhood with people mistaking them for twins. They are each other's best friends and have a truly beautiful relationship. She was heartbroken for herself and me, but nothing could describe the pain she felt for her brother. And there she was with her perfect, healthy baby. It breaks my heart how hard that must have been for her. I wasn't equipped or able to help her through those feelings, but part of this book is to remind you to check in on fam-ily members along the way. For many of them, their grief is two-fold. My mother-in-law and father-in-law were watching their son break with pain, but they had also lost their first grandson. Their grief, and my sister-in-law's pain, was also very real.

I am very much aware that I was lucky enough to have a family who put their feelings aside to try to hold us up. That is absolutely not the case for many, many bereaved parents. Some parents can feel like there is no-one to turn to. They may also feel like no one else can possibly understand what they are going through.

It is important to acknowledge that there are organisations who offer help, but it can be terribly limited and not always appropriate to the loss at hand. I have listed some of the more broadly known organisations in the *Resources* part of this book.

For example, if a child has died an especially traumatic death such as a road traffic accident, there is specialist support available, and parents in that situation may find it valuable to talk with other parents whose children have died in the same kind of way.

That is not to say that all parents who lose a child will always want to talk to other bereaved parents. For some, that may just feel too real to begin with. They must do these things in their own time.

Bereaved parents will often talk of *The Club*. This is the club that you join when your child dies. I have been a musician my whole life, I have been in some truly awful clubs, but this is by far the worst club I've ever known! It's a terrible club. No one wants to join; we don't want to be in it, and we don't want anyone else to be in it. Sadly, we accrue new members all the time, but we so wish that the membership wasn't building. The cost of joining is just far too expensive.

Members of *The Club* talk to each other in a way that we are unable to talk to other people. There is an honesty that bereaved parents have with each other, a way of speaking openly that we can't have with anyone else, including family members. Often when we speak about our children to people externally, we will talk generally and not go into detail, especially around the more traumatic parts, such as our child's last moments. With our fellow *Club* members, we know we can share *all* the parts of our child's life and death, and we don't have any responsibility to protect anyone's feelings. We can voice our truest emotions, including our anger and frustration at our situation and also with those around us.

This is a good place to point out too that just because someone is bereaved doesn't mean that they will be the right support for another bereaved parent. It also doesn't mean that they will automatically have the emotional energy to support someone else. I recently had someone message me as part of a group message on social media introducing me to his friend, also on the group, who had just lost her child because "he thought it would be good for her to meet someone else who had lost a child." He didn't reach out to me before doing this, nor did he warn this mum that he was going to do it. I am often one of the first people to reach out to someone I see who has had a loss, but I always check where I am at first in myself. I don't always have the energy for the emotional labour it takes. No matter what, I will always re-live Dexter's death as a result of those kinds of conversations, and that is okay, but I need to know I have the energy for it at that moment. This message came within days of his 16th birthday. I was not okay.

One thing we don't do in *The Club* is judge anyone's entry criteria. We don't have a strict dress code of no trainers. Of course, we'd prefer you weren't there, but we have no say over whether you get in. If we did, no one would ever have to join us again. And tracksuit pants would be completely acceptable.

Whilst we are part of *The Club*, that doesn't mean that we will all think the same way or deal with things in the same way. I know parents who would rather not talk about it, and I know parents who seldom speak of anything else. I know parents who do not want to know other bereaved parents, and I know parents who only want to know other bereaved parents. It is a personal choice and whilst you may not always understand it, it is best that you respect it. We are changed from who we once were, and we might need space to work out who we are going to be from this point on.

WISDOM NUGGETS

❖ Grief is not comparable. Please remember this when you think the age of a child makes a difference to how much validity their parent's grief has.

❖ Don't start sentences with the phrase "At least." The inference here is that things could somehow be worse. Nothing is worse than this right now. Please acknowledge that.

❖ There is no "bright side" in this. There can be things that can come out of the person you may become after your child dies, but, especially in those first days, there is barely light, let alone anything "bright."

❖ If appropriate, help find support that fits with the parent's needs. I have listed more specific places of •If support for families based on their individual needs in the Resources part of this book and my website. Parents may not want to access it, but it is important to inform them.

❖ If you do want to connect people, please check that both parties have the emotional capacity for that. Remember we are all individuals and therefore, we will be dealing with things in our own, individual, ways.

CHAPTER TWO

"I Know How You Feel."

"My feelings can perhaps be imagined, but they can hardly be described."

Yann Martel

You really, really don't.

I could meet a mother whose child died of the same severity of Zellweger syndrome as Dexter, at 4 weeks and 3 days, and I STILL would not know how she feels.

Our feelings are shaped by the experiences we have already had in our lives, so no two people can have the same feelings just by default.

It is, however, one of the phrases that is said to me more than any other. As human beings we want connection, and we will try anything in a moment of pain to help someone understand that we are there for them. That we get them, and we know what they are going through. Often, the phrase comes with a qualifying reason that they know, and here is where the territory gets sticky.

Death touches all of us sadly. There will be many emotions, and "stages" as illustrated by the Kubler-Ross Model.[6] These are the ones you may have heard of. Denial. Anger. Bargaining. Depression. Acceptance.

In 1960, Dr Elizabeth Kubler-Ross published the book "On Death and Dying." Since then, it has been one of the most significant publications to outline the psychological effects of grief. It has helped millions of

---

6   https://www.ncbi.nlm.nih.gov/books/NBK507885/

people have at least some kind of understanding of what it is they're going through. Although it was written for grieving someone, it has long been adapted and used to help decipher bereavement.

We need to talk about one emotional response that isn't on that list. Shock. Even when you know death is inevitable, the shock of it happening can be debilitating. Shock is not denial. It is the disbelief that this has happened. It is the blacking out of all light. It is the unending belief that life is over. It can cause not only emotional response but physical as well. Rapid heartbeat, loss of appetite, shortness of breath. These are physical manifestations of shock. They can be in the moment of death, but can also return many, many times within the first months of loss, and even further down the line. The acknowledgement of it can help immensely.

I am not criticising the model; it is crucial information. People like things to be laid out for them. They like a road map or a plan. The Kubler-Ross Model provides that. It doesn't claim to be all-encompassing, it never did, but universally it has been interpreted as the definitive way that people *SHOULD* handle grief. Grief is not linear, and the model never said it was.

All these stages are real and important. They are all present and accounted for when you are going through loss. Sometimes, they all show themselves quickly, but often they are spread apart. Most of what we will experience will probably fall under the umbrella of each of these stages. What it doesn't mean, however, is that every feeling a bereaved parent has WILL fall under the umbrella. That is an important distinction. Grief is like a fingerprint, entirely unique. It is personal. It is lonely and isolating and our own experience of grief previously shapes how we deal with others and their experience. Although you may have found comparable emotions, the way you experience them will be completely different.

I have known my best friend in Australia, Tildie and her Mum, Elesa (affectionately known as "Mrs A"), for most of my life. I think I met them when I was about 7 years old, and they have been a part of my life ever since. Tildie was beautiful and popular and despite what that combination usually means in Hollywood teen movies, she was also really kind. Tildie and her mum were close. Incredibly so, and they were best friends. Mrs A was one of the funniest, kindest people I've ever met, so I know how Tildie saw her as her best friend. Mrs A knew much more about my complicated home situation than most, and yet, she seemed to have this sixth sense that I was somehow special. She always made me feel I could be someone and she always made it clear that she believed in me. Many years later, when things started to take shape in my career, she would say to me "You always had the power my dear" a quote from the film classic The Wizard of Oz. She was pretty much at the top of the list of people I desperately wanted to make proud. I now sport this phrase in tattoo form on my right forearm.

Not long after Dexter had died, Mrs A visited me in the UK, only to return home to Australia to be diagnosed with aggressive triple-negative breast cancer. This one is an extra nasty form of breast cancer, with a 5-year survival rate of around 12%. It is more aggressive, and tumours have a faster growth rate than other breast cancers, so it is particularly difficult to treat. Although she fought and fought, sadly she died on May 31, 2018, at 69 years old. It was utterly devastating and Tildie was broken.

My own mother and I had a fractured relationship with much of my childhood seeing me raised in the care of others and the state. We weren't estranged but we did not have a conventional or "normal" mother/daughter relationship. My mum was my first experience of glamour. She was the most beautiful woman I had ever seen, and I worshipped her. Long auburn hair and a Marilyn Monroe-shaped figure, she turned heads everywhere she went. She was a singer and probably the biggest reason that I was ecstatic when I learnt I could sing at the age of 14. I desperately wanted her to notice me, to love me, and I thought that would do it.

Sadly, alongside all that beauty and charisma came a whole host of mental and emotional issues and she spent her lifetime suffering. Sadly, she could be unpredictable, selfish and cruel at times as a result. When I was 11 she left me with my paternal grandparents, one of the kindest things she ever did, and I saw her rarely after that. We spoke intermittently and I hoped over the years that we would be able to develop some semblance of a relationship, a place I had gotten to after many years of feeling as though I was without a mother, and not unfairly so. Tragically, my mother died suddenly by her own hand in 2008.

Tildie and I both lost our mums, but my feelings around the loss of my mother are vastly different to Tildie's based on my experiences. It's not to say any one of us had it worse than the other (see Chapter One), but whilst I could try to understand Tildie's pain, I couldn't know what it felt like to lose a mother who had been close in the way that she and Mrs A were. Arguably I had grieved for my mother in my teenage years a little already, but even that wasn't the same. I did not, and cannot know, how Tildie felt. I understand why her feelings run so deep and why she is still in so much pain over her mother's death, even though I, sadly, didn't experience that same kind of pain over my own mother's death. Of course, I am terribly sad that she died, and I grieve for the woman I never truly got to know, but I am almost grieving the death of an idea rather than the person completely.

Leading with the words "I know how you feel" once again makes this loss about someone other than the bereaved parent. It doesn't leave space for us to tell you honestly how we feel. It is said to be empathic, but it will often shut down a parent as it can feel invalidating. Remember that we are lonely in this. We don't want a single person in the world to ever feel this heartache. It is THAT painful. In our hearts at that moment, it's not unusual to feel that no one ever has felt pain like we are feeling. When someone comes along telling you they "know" it can make us feel like you aren't listening to how much pain we are actually in, even though that is not your intention.

Make no mistake, I never EVER want anyone to have any closer knowledge of what it feels like to lose a child. I don't want anyone to experience that pain at all. Sadly, however, I can't stop that it happens, but I do want you to recognise that the isolation a bereaved parent can feel can be made worse by words not thought through by those around them.

Ultimately what I am saying is that whilst you don't know how someone feels, if you're willing to listen, they can share with you how they do feel and you may be able to help them reconcile some of those feelings, even just by listening. Listening, and allowing us to feel what we are feeling, without comparison or judgement, is one of the most powerful things you can do to help. Yes, practical things help (we will cover this throughout the book) but your presence, your willingness to sit with your own discomfort and upset to be near us and have us feel less alone, that is the thing we need most.

I'm an empath, so I can't help but feel like I need to help you through this bit too, so I am going to give you one rule to follow after you have sat with a bereaved parent and listened. Talk to someone else. Tell them how you feel. Share your anger, denial and shock. You are allowed to, and will, feel pain. You need to ensure your well-being to be able to truly support someone else. It is just a little bit easier on us if you don't ask us to be your support as well.

Oftentimes bereaved parents will go into a protection mode with people they love. It is why we will often only share more intimate details of our child's journey with members of *The Club*. We love you. We don't want to see you hurt. We know it hurts you to see us in pain. We are going to do everything we can to ensure your emotional safety in all of this if we can. That includes not telling you some of the trauma we may have experienced. We know you may feel you can hear it all, but believe me, you don't always want to. Honestly, there are some things you don't need to know. So don't be offended if you feel we haven't completely opened up to you. Sometimes it's just too hard. Sometimes watching people you love in pain is the hardest thing you can do.

Hands down, the person whose reaction broke me the most was my father-in-law. He is the strongest, most stoic northern Englishman I have ever met. After his father, died in his early 40s, not long after returning from World War 2, he had to leave school at 15 and get work with the National Coal Board to help support his widowed mother. He eventually retired as a successful business owner with a love and dedication to his family I have always admired.

He and my mother-in-law were in the room when we were told Dexter was going to die. They were as shocked at that moment as we were. They had to digest this information as we did, and all the while, they had to watch us completely fall apart. I think in hindsight, I am selfishly glad it wasn't us who had to tell them, but I also know that we were unable to offer them any comfort at a time when they were also being given the information that their only grandson, was going to die. I do wish I could have done that for them, but I am also very aware that I am so fortunate that I was spared that incredibly difficult conversation. That isn't the case for most bereaved families.

Once we were given the news, we were all able to go and see Dexter in his special care crib, in pairs. My husband and my father-in-law went together so I didn't see his reaction at first, but later, as we were given a room where we could spend time together as a family, I saw him break down. It was the most heartbreaking thing I have ever witnessed. Even today the memory brings me to tears. After we took Dexter home, he set about doing all the practical things he could to get the whole family through, and I mean all of them. He made a feeding contraption that meant we could hold Dexter whilst feeding him (he was fed through a nasal gastric tube) and know his milk was flowing properly through the tube. He also practically renovated our house! He did whatever he needed to keep busy and ensure his family was getting through. These days, whilst he might not talk openly about his memories of Dexter, he never shies away from hearing his name or us talking about him.

Not to forget my mother-in-law in all this. She got me through those first few weeks and is hands down the best grandmother all four of her grandchildren could have asked for! Although if you ask the grandkids, she has never let them have enough sweets! Even now, she has a quiet way of making sure Dexter is always a part of our lives, with a kind word or gesture when I need it. On birthdays and anniversaries, hers is always the first text of the day, flowers are always left, and hugs are given. She is the perfect example of actions being as powerful as words.

We know that this is all hurting you too. At that moment, however, we will rarely have the capacity to get you, along with ourselves through it. This is why we need you to take charge of your grief at this point. In time, we can possibly talk about how you felt, but even if we don't, believe me when I say, we will have thought about it. That thinking will frequently lead us back to the feelings of guilt that many bereaved parents feel concerning their loved ones. We never wanted you to go through this either.

I remember the first words out of my mouth when we were given Dexter's diagnosis and subsequent prognosis. As we sat in a tiny room at the hospital, we were told there was no hope. Our son was absolutely going to die. There was no treatment available, he was unsavable. I turned to my family and said, "I'm so sorry, this is all my fault."

It wasn't my fault. It was no one's fault. It was a blip in the system. A horrible circumstance that my husband and I would both carry and then pass on a defective gene. It was so rare that no one would ever have seen it coming. But somehow, I felt responsible. I am his mother. I carried him. How could I not have protected him? How could I have let this happen? Of course, I know in the logical part of my brain, that none of those feelings are based on any truth, but that's the thing about these situations. They can see us have the most irrational of thoughts.

That day we entered the phase called *pre-emptive* or *anticipatory* grief. That is the grief that someone starts to feel when they know that death is imminent. That "imminence" may however be within days, months or even years. We were told we could expect a few months at best, but at that moment, we started to grieve. That's not to say we were seeing it as that. We didn't even have a moment to think about the future and what we wouldn't be doing, we were too busy learning to look after our son who had severe and complex special needs.

It's important to recognise that whilst we should never compare grief, there are different types of grief. Ultimately, they all land us in the same state of grieving. It is important to know what they are and to acknowledge that those differences exist. We often invalidate someone's grief simply because we don't understand it. As a society, we interpret grief as something that is only experienced by those directly involved in a death. There are, however, many types of grief that can affect us in more ways than we might think.

Perhaps the events of September 11 are a good example of this. Many people weren't directly affected by what happened on that day, but many, many people felt what we know as *collective* grief because of it. This is where a group, community or area feel the direct effect of the death of others, regardless of their relationship to the person or people who have died. Many native New Yorkers talk of this kind of grief after this fateful day.

Another example is *disenfranchised* grief. This is often experienced by what are often called "rainbow babies." This is the name many people call children born after a loss. Rainbow babies will often grow up with the knowledge that there was a child before them who is no longer here, but they are often overlooked as having any grief around that loss as they didn't come until after the child who died or were very young when their sibling died so they have little or no memory of them.

My youngest son Arlo came into our lives, screaming, in July 2008, 9 months after Dexter died. Arlo makes me feel like I have two boys at home! He is funny and caring and challenging, and he hasn't yet learned to read a room! He is also very aware that his brother died of a genetic condition and that we got pregnant with him very quickly after his death. He knows that we are over-protective, helicopter parents because our fears of losing a child, although in very different circumstances, were realised. He accepts and acknowledges why, even if he does find it annoying at times. That said, we are incredibly close because of this.

When Arlo was small, he would say that he wished he had his brother to play with. He would often say that he wished Dexter was here. It would break my heart. When he was about 12, the first real understanding of what it meant that his brother had died, seemed to come to him for the first time. He felt real heartache. He felt like he had missed out on something that he was watching so many of his friends, and family members, have. A closeness to a confidante with whom he could share life and growing up. As adults, I think we can often forget how strong emotions run as teenagers. Arlo's heartbreak to him isn't about the physical loss of his brother. It is about what he has missed out on, and consequently, because we decided to not risk pregnancy again, what he could never have. His pain *is* grief.

In supporting grief, it helps to understand it a little more, and the many ways, that it can show itself. We may not always know why, but it's important to not question its validity.

WISDOM NUGGETS

Here are some helpful phrases if you don't feel you know what to say.

❖ I don't know how you feel but I am here to listen if you want to talk.

❖ I don't know how you feel but I understand that this must be so incredibly difficult. Would you like to talk about it?

❖ I don't know how you feel but I can understand/recognise some of the emotions you may be experiencing. Do you want to talk through any of them?

❖ Just simply, "Would you like to talk about how you are feeling?"

❖ I would like to hear about how this feels for you if you want to talk about it.

❖ I can't make this better, but I am here if you want to talk, or if you just want to sit and say nothing.

❖ Is there anything I can do for you?

❖ Ask everyone in the family what they need, including siblings. Their grief is also very real.

CHAPTER THREE

"Are You Not Over It Yet?"

"Grief changes shape, but it never ends."

Keanu Reeves.

I wish someone could tell me what the correct amount of time to mourn the death of my child is. I mean, people seem to know the answer when they say this phrase, but not one of them has been able to give me an actual date yet.

Believe me, if you could have told me that by 3 years and 45 days exactly, my grief would be over, I would have given you all the money I make for the rest of my life! (Given that I'm an artist, that would be about £300 and an extensive collection of shoes, but you could have it all!) We don't know how long grief lasts, the only thing we do know is that we can't avoid it and it can come knocking back on our door at any time.

I quoted Keanu Reeves at the beginning of this chapter for two reasons. One, I live in desperate hope that either he or Dave Grohl will finally one day realise I am missing from their lives and come for me.

Two, more importantly, because of the loss of his daughter Ava, who was stillborn in 1999 (sadly her mother Jennifer died in a tragic accident only 2 years later). Reeves talks in interviews of wondering what daily life would be like were they still here. What might they have done together? He says he misses all the great things they will never be. So again, for any bereaved parent, famous or otherwise, what we will never have, never allows us to "get over it."

We tried once as a society to quantify grief.[7] In Victorian times when a husband died, his widow was given a 2-year period in which to mourn. She would wear heavy black clothing[8] (to the best of her income), and she was also instructed on what social events she could take part in. A widow was not able to attend pleasurable events, such as balls during this time for example but was expected in church. Conversely, when a child died, the mother was allowed a 1-year mourning period. I'm not sure who thought husbands warranted a longer time than children. Clearly, the person who came up with this wasn't married.

I often hear people say about this era, "Yes, but children died more often then." Yes, they did. We didn't have the medical knowledge we do now, but parents were still parents. I don't think our ancestors felt children were any more expendable then than they are now. Perhaps it's our collective mentality trying to reconcile how parents could have experienced so much loss during those times, but I certainly can't imagine a world where even if you knew there were many reasons that your child may die, you wouldn't still love that child with every fibre of your being.

We all know there are risks for children. We are terrified of them. As a bereaved parent, we will often hear other parents say that they don't know what they would do if something happened to their child. We have acute hearing for those sorts of phrases. We also don't know what you would do but we wouldn't expect your grieving to be done and over with quickly. With open arms, we would welcome you into *The Club* and try to reassure you that sometime, at some point, it won't hurt like this 24 hours a day.

I think that a major part of the issue with this is that we love a time frame. We like knowing when something will finish, especially when it's painful. It is usually the first question of a painful medical procedure; how long will it take and how long will it take to heal? These incidentally are my first words to my dentist every time I see him. No one likes to be

7   https://www.thefrickpittsburgh.org/Story-Memory-and-Mourning-Death-in-the-Gilded-Age#:~:text=The%20recommended%20length%20of%20time,to%20remarry%20more%20than%20widows.
8   https://pubmed.ncbi.nlm.nih.gov/18507326/

in pain. (I also don't really like my dentist! He is actually pretty nice to be fair, and he really does tolerate my penchant for the dramatic). We want everything hard to be quick and painless. The grief over the death of your child is long and arduous and painful and eventually, often dismissed. It doesn't fit with what other people want to have to think about.

It can be easy to think that as time goes on, we *should* be okay by now. We *should* have learned to navigate the world again. Remember this is a world that shows immediate discomfort when we mention our child's name. A world that thinks that if we just get back on with things like work and social events, we will be fine. A world that thinks if we just have another baby, we can replace the pain with love, and everything will be okay.

That's not a world we want to be in any longer. For some, that may be a literal feeling but for most, I mean it metaphorically. Many of us are scrambling to understand a world where our child would be taken from us and where we are expected to be the same as we were before.

I won't say that time helps but, for me, in time, it began to feel less visceral. Again, *for me*. For those first few months, I could only handle one day at a time. For a long time waking up. I could still smell him. Holding his clothes and blankets, would feel like he was in my arms once again. Inevitably, those smells began to fade, and I would find myself distraught that I couldn't simply lock them away in a plastic bag forever that I could open daily and be transported back into a world in which he was still alive.

After a painful first year, one of what should have been so many joyful "firsts," I felt I was able to do things like return to work (I actually did that after four months - a move I would later regret). By this point, I also discovered I was expecting another baby, but instead of feeling overjoyed, I was going through a worrying pregnancy that I simply could not believe would result in a healthy baby. I was counting the days until he was born so I could hear him cry. That pregnancy brought about a whole new set of complications, not only because we have a genetic defect, but because it seemed to indicate to other people that I was fine. I was, according to the rest of the world, "over Dexter."

[34]

As soon as we returned to some semblance of normality, the world assumed that we were okay when the reality was that we were just trying to get by. We had a mortgage and bills to pay. I couldn't just stop working, and neither could Chris. We had to get back into the flow of life, even though in many ways, it had continued to stand still. Our grief was like a dam, stopping any joy from getting through. Both of our employers were exceptional throughout this time, and neither of us felt pressured to get back to work, but I shudder to think of the many people who return to work because it can mean the difference between food on the table or not. I did feel like I was lucky enough to have a choice, but I fully appreciate I am in the minority.

Losing a child is a life sentence. I can assure you, that no matter how much time passes we will never forget our child or the pain we feel because of their death. On occasion, we can think about them, and the pain will pass over quickly, allowing us to bask in the memory or the photograph that took us back to that moment in the first place. At other times, without any word of warning, it can feel like we are right back there, unable to breathe, suffocating under the heartbreak, as though it was yesterday. It is difficult to explain these moments because, more often than not, it has taken us completely by surprise and we are once again experiencing extreme grief in every part of our body. Sometimes it's a smell, or it could be a place. At other times, its watching and celebrating a life event that our child isn't able to be a part of. Mostly, it's not anything other than our brain reminding us that we are missing a core part of our being.

I wish I could tell any bereaved parent that eventually this will stop happening, but it is important to acknowledge that we will never stop having these moments. Eventually, they may not seem to happen quite so often but that is more likely because we are distracted with life, and other things, and not because grief doesn't lay in wait like spinach in your teeth, ready to appear just before you see the hot, popular guy from high school at your 25-year reunion.

Dexter was born on September 12, and he died on October 15 at 4 weeks and 3 days old. The months of September to October are fraught with emotion for me. I didn't notice it for a while, but after a few years, I could see a pattern emerging during that time. The first thing I recall is being overly emotional about everything. I would find it harder to control my emotions in all sorts of situations and I found myself seeing the worst in most scenarios. I'm a pretty pragmatic person. I like to find solutions and I don't like to wallow. I can see the value in feeling emotions deeply, but I'm an "action" person, so I couldn't understand why, to my mind, I was being so irrational.

The second thing to note is that I became unbearably over-protective toward Arlo. He wouldn't be allowed to do much out of school during that time if he wasn't overseen by me or his dad, and in every scenario, I could imagine danger. I could see it in my mind, in graphic detail, that he would get hurt. There were times I would make him walk on the inside of the pavement, as I was convinced a car would run onto the pavement at any point and he would die. I wasn't just worried this would happen, in my mind's eye, I could vividly see it play out. It was a rational fear but my belief that it was absolutely going to happen was irrational.

After a while, and a conversation with my husband, where he admitted similar feelings, I recognised that there was a pattern I hadn't seen before. It was most often during the weeks between Dexter's birthday and anniversary that I would drive myself crazy with scenarios in which we would lose Arlo. Don't get me wrong, I fear for him every day, like any parent, and we have certainly taken longer than many of his friends' parents to allow him to do things away from us, but I am not talking about usual parental fear. I'm talking about debilitating fear that would see me hysterical at the idea of him leaving my sight.

The most common manifestation would see me re-living Dexter's death over and over in my head, and in some of those replays, his face would be replaced by Arlo's. It was my mind playing horrific tricks on me, but it took me a long time to piece it all together and even longer to start to open up to people that I may not be at my best during that period.

Now, I am 100% that person who will tell everyone quite openly, "It's that time of year. Bear with me." Over the years I have surrounded myself with friends and family who have listened, so I don't need to explain myself. Since I started acknowledging the time frame and my feelings around it, it easier to get through, but now I make sure to do plenty of things that recognise it as a tougher time for me. I try to cut back on work or deadlines (this rarely happens by the way – I am self-employed!) and I make time to talk about Dexter and what he means to us. Celebrating him at this time feels like the best possible way to make sure that my heart, and my head, are looked after even though I know that it won't take the pain away.

At the end of the day, a parent will never "get over" the death of their child. The sooner everyone understands that the better.

Again, I think it's helpful to guide you through some of the language or actions that may be helpful or comforting to your loved ones around the time it takes to grieve.

WISDOM NUGGETS

❖ Acknowledge that you do not expect them to be "healed." Let them tell you why it still feels like yesterday for them. This is important for a bereaved parent regardless of how long ago their loss was. This grief never goes away. We don't magically forget that our child lived and then died just because it was x number of years ago.

❖ Reassure them that whatever point wherever they are at in their journey, that is right for them and there is no pre-determined time frame as far as you are concerned.

❖ Send them quotes that you find around grief and grieving, that show you are thinking of them and the journey they are on. You can also send words such as "thinking of you and (their child's name) today." I can't explain how powerfully comforting it is to know someone has thought about you and acknowledged your child at such an important time and why you are in so much pain.

[37]

❖ Try to remember that any time can be a "bad time" for a bereaved parent. Just because it might not seem obvious to someone else, doesn't mean there is no significance for them.

CHAPTER FOUR

"You Can Always Have Another One."

*"Just because a parent's arms are now full, in no way does
it make their heart grieve any less for the little one no longer here."*

Zoe Clark-Coates

People said this to me. A lot.

You are talking about my child. A human being. I carried this child.
Loved this child the moment I knew about him. I couldn't just replace
him, and everything would be okay.

For me, and for reasons that belong in another book, it took a long time
to allow myself to enjoy my pregnancy, but by the time I had that first
scan, I was all in. Therefore, the subsequent loss of it was traumatic and
shocking. It did, however, make me question the societal expectation
that we don't announce pregnancy until after the "safe" amount of time
designated as being three months.

There is no medical reason that we wait this time. I will repeat. There
is *no* medical reason that we are advised to wait this time. The twelve-
week scan in pregnancy is for very specific reasons. It checks your dates,
makes sure the heart is beating, checks how many babies are in there
and looks at very specific data to ensure there are no issues with the developing foetus. We wait solely because it has become a societal norm.
That said, no one has to tell anyone until they want to. It is an entirely
personal decision, but it should be made with all the relevant information.

Sadly, once we make it through this part of the pregnancy, a happy outcome isn't guaranteed. Before 12 weeks, loss at this point is termed a miscarriage.[9] Between 12 and 24 weeks of pregnancy, it is considered a late miscarriage. Somewhere between 1-5 in 100 pregnancies end in late miscarriage. After 20 weeks, this is considered stillbirth and it is not as uncommon as people may think. In the UK, 1 in every 250 pregnancies results in a stillborn child. That is a far bigger number than you may have realised. To break it down for you, that is around 8 families a day giving birth to a child who will never take their first breath.

The first time we found out we were pregnant; we were travelling across the USA, driving along Route 66 with 11 of our closest friends. We had arrived in St Louis, and I felt dreadful. We weren't necessarily "trying" for a baby, but we had said we would start thinking about it. I found myself at a Walgreens on the third morning of our trip buying a pregnancy test and looking shocked at the double lines indicating it was positive! As we gathered for breakfast, we said we had something to tell everyone, at which point our friend Tony said, "You're pregnant" and everyone laughed. Until they noticed we weren't laughing as hard. It was congratulations all around and me realising that the planned trip to Vegas at the end of the holiday was going to be a real drag!

As our friends were there right at the beginning (not the actual beginning!) of this pregnancy, it meant they were invested, so telling them when it all went wrong was difficult, but they were unbelievably supportive. Because of this, I saw the true value of having the right support in miscarriage. Of course, I still felt alone, but I felt acknowledged, and we were very open once we got pregnant again. We continue to have a strong bond with this group of friends. It feels like we have all experienced so much together. Thankfully they are still very much a part of our lives, with four of them officially assigned as doting godparents to the boys.

A loss, at any point of pregnancy, can have a profound effect on families. What is crucial to remember in all of this is that they are all grieving. Their grief is real and valid and it's not for anyone to question that. Once

---

9   https://www.nidirect.gov.uk/articles/miscarriage-stillbirth-and-ectopic-pregnancy

again, comparing helps no one. It can leave many people alone in their loss, often without any access to therapeutic interventions such as counselling.

People will deal with these losses in different ways. It is such a personal journey. For me, and I will re-emphasise this, for *me*, my miscarriage was painful and heart-breaking, but before I knew it, I was presented with another baby, who I was told was going to die soon, so I have always felt that all my grief was kind of rolled into one. I didn't have much time to think about or reconcile that miscarriage, but I am sure it has been a part of my journey.

That said, I was pretty preoccupied.

For many parents, it could be one of many losses or the beginning of many losses. I am sad to say that I know many women who have had multiple miscarriages. According to Tommys.org (the baby loss charity), to have any access to medical investigation, many women may have to have as many as three consecutive losses. Additionally, very often, when you have experienced this kind of number, the unlikelihood of you carrying a baby to term becomes greater. It may also lead to being told that pregnancy will never be on the cards for you. This is where we can see one of those other forms of grief at play, *disenfranchised* grief. The grief for something that you have never had. People can easily dismiss how important having children is for some people, so it is impossible to know the pain associated with being told it will never happen for you. It once again seems a terribly lonely place to be, and it is so horribly sad that it is rarely acknowledged.

My point in all of this is that life after loss is a strange place to be and no matter what got you there, it isn't for someone else to decide how we should be dealing with it.

Having another child can make you reflect heavily on the loss you have experienced up to that point. This can be a difficult set of emotions to get your head around. It can also make you very fearful for the well-being of the child you have. To others, those fears can be seen as irrational, but they are based on a very real set of concerns. Dismissing them helps no one.

People would so readily ask us when we were going to "try again." I kept wanting to scream in their face that they seemed to have forgotten what had happened. I know they just wanted us to be happy; it was never asked without love, but it didn't help, as it made me feel that people had forgotten about Dexter and that they didn't feel his death mattered any more.

Rather embarrassingly, we got pregnant a month after Dexter died. I say embarrassingly, as I was mortified that people would know we were having sex! After all, our son had just died. I am generalising here of course, but men and women often grieve in very different ways and whilst women will often want to speak of their loss as much as possible, men will often seek physical closeness. In one of life's cruel ironies, Chris and I have never had an issue getting pregnant, rather, we just have trouble having a healthy baby. I used to say we couldn't pass on the stairs without him knocking me up. I was pregnant for pretty much 3 years, but it felt like it had really been about 15. The wine industry almost went bankrupt!

We say now that we were so lucky to get pregnant when we did because even in those first weeks, we had discussed the idea of trying again, and already both agreed that we would probably not take the risk. Zellweger's is an autosomal recessive disorder, so both Chris and I carry it. We have a 1 in 2 chance of passing it to any child we have and then there is a 1 in 4 chance that child will develop the disorder that we carry. There was a 1 in 50 million chance that we would meet, and both carry this defective gene. Suffice it to say that we are not people who are confident in our numbers. So having another child was taking an enormous risk.

I genuinely thought that with how distraught we were, pregnancy just wouldn't happen. We were grieving so hard. We had taken a trip to Norway to spend time with our family and our new niece and once again, unbeknownst to us, we came home pregnant. We had actually gotten pregnant with Dexter on a previous trip to Norway. Turns out the Norse gods liked to bless us with sons!

Once again, the hardest part of the pregnancy was telling everyone. We knew just how much fear there would be for our loved ones this time. We also had to have very early testing to see if this baby had the same disease as Dexter. At 8 weeks in, I had the intrusive CVS (chorionic villus sampling) test, and we had the excruciating wait until 20 weeks, to find out that this baby boy was going to be free and clear of Zellweger's. There was a collective sigh of relief amongst everyone we knew when the tests came back to say he was perfectly healthy.

As he had almost no muscle tone, Dexter was unable to cry like other babies so we knew that normal crying would indicate this baby was okay at birth. At 38 weeks, by planned caesarean section, Arlo Dexter was born. He came out screaming, so we knew immediately that he was going to be alright - and a handful.

We made the difficult decision to not try for more children after Arlo. The idea of passing such a horrible disease on to another child was just too much for us to think about. We had lucked out with him, cheated the odds in our minds, and we just didn't feel like we could be so lucky again. I underestimated the grief I would have in not being able to have another child. It didn't feel like a choice for us. It felt like the only decision we could make. I knew that I wouldn't be able to terminate a pregnancy knowing that the baby could be born and survive for up to 6 months. But I knew I couldn't live through the death of another child. So, there was no choice.

All of this is not to say that you can never ask us the question. Perhaps though, you should ask yourself why you are asking in the first place. If you take the chance, are you prepared for the answer? If you're not, don't ask. My life's work and passion are to encourage people to talk about their grief, so I hope for a world where those of us who have experienced these losses can be much more open. It is time to stop hiding these conversations away. It is time to stop hiding our grief.

WISDOM NUGGETS

❖ Ask if they want to talk about it. Listen if they do.

❖ If announcing a pregnancy to a person who has lost a child, for experienced miscarriage) take some time to tell them privately, giving them time to digest and reconcile their feelings. We will be happy for you, we just might be upset for a moment first. Please allow us to have this moment.

❖ Help them memorialise. (See Part Two)

❖ Discourage joke pregnancy announcements. If you see people doing this, tell them not to and why.

❖ Recognise the validity of their grief. It is not for anyone to say how long a pregnancy should last before it was "valid" in that person's mind.

❖ In the case of stillbirth, say their child's name. Recognise their existence. Acknowledge birthdays and special occasions. Also, remember that "firsts" can often be very difficult. Their grief is not just the now, it is also for a future taken away.

A NOTE ON MISCARRIAGE

The idea that having a baby is just rainbows and light is ludicrous. Especially now that we are in an age where we are far more likely to hear about the struggle to have children. I thoroughly welcome the openness that is changing around having children (and choosing not to have children) and the highlighting that it isn't always as simple as deciding what you're going to do and, VOILA! A baby!

Pregnancy is a minefield. I don't want to take the magic away from it, but it is fraught with danger and risk, and we need to consider these things when we flippantly talk to people about having babies.

Firstly, in a sort of related Public Service Announcement; Not All People Want Babies. So stop asking. Or ask in a way that isn't as intrusive as "When is it your turn?"

These days we know now more than ever the prevalence of miscarriage (believed to be as high as 1 in 4 pregnancies according to the National Institute for Health and Care Excellence). However, this isn't the only reason someone might not have a baby. Infertility, financial considerations, family issues. It's just not something you can 1— know by looking at someone. When we barrel into conversations about when someone is going to "try again" it is worth taking a beat to think about what you are going to ask.

For my husband and I, our first pregnancy together went horribly wrong. It ended with a surgical procedure and me peeing into a cup every week for 2 years and sending it off to a hospital in Sheffield. (This was on account of having a partial molar pregnancy that I miscarried with before I got pregnant with Dexter). We were also told to wait a minimum of three months before we tried again and we trotted off to Norway for Christmas, only to come back, unknowingly, pregnant.

After our miscarriage, my sister-in-law had fallen pregnant and for her, the tough bit was telling us given what we had just been through. I have to say, we could do with a whole lot more conversations around miscarriage and the complexity of that loss, but also about how we navigate around those people who have them.

We need to stop pretending that miscarriage isn't a serious loss. We are getting better, but nowhere near where we need to be. Some pregnancies are unplanned, some are happy surprises, some are incredibly planned, and some only exist because of continuous, and massive, clinical intervention. Yet, as a society, we still seem to dismiss the loss of a pregnancy as something that isn't something that needs grieving.

Whatever headspace you are in when you get pregnant, it can be a very isolating time. Not always in a bad way, but you spend a lot of time in your head, weirdly 1— knowing that you are never alone for this time. Acknowledging that a human being is growing inside you is a strange sensation. It is only natural for some to develop an 0 indescribable bond with that human. (This, of course, won't be true for everyone. I am being very general for the sake of brevity.)

There are now some incredible organizations and individuals talking about miscarriage who are worth looking in to if you are supporting a loved one after a miscarriage. I have listed these in the Resources part of this book.

CHAPTER FIVE

"At Least It Was Just A Baby."

"A new baby is like the beginning of all things – wonder, hope, a dream of possibilities"

Eda J. LeShan

There is this very strange and dark thing that someone does when they utter these words. They reinforce the idea that there is a magical age in which society decides that a child's life matters.

I should really start by saying that I don't believe that anyone says this with that in mind. Most people are thinking, "Well, at least you didn't know them better." However, bringing a child into the world means bringing a lifetime of hopes and dreams, and when they die, it is also the death of these things. It is far-reaching and involves a future that has now been denied.

The problem with any phrase that starts with "at least" is that it implies that "it is okay because….". The inference is that it doesn't matter; that our child isn't important because they hadn't yet contributed to the world in a way that others think is valuable.

I have often wondered why we place differing values as we do, and perhaps there is a systemic element.

In Victorian England, having a baby was playing with dice.[10] Their

---

10   https://www.ons.gov.uk/peoplepopulationandcommunity/birthsdeathsand-marriages/lifeexpectancies/articles/howhaslifeexpectancychangedover-time/2015-09-09

chance of survival to 1 year was only 30%. 43% of children would not live past 5 and if they did survive to 10, they still only had a 60% chance of living into adulthood. Thanks to advancements in medicine and hygiene, those numbers now are vastly different, but it makes you wonder if the fear of our child dying within that first year is something that sits in the memory of our DNA.

In 1836, the Death Registrations Act was passed in Parliament.[11] This meant in England, the registration of a death was a legal requirement for all who died. A centralised network was set up alongside it. It wasn't until 1837 that the cause of death was even required on a death certificate. Alongside this column were sex, age and occupation. Up until 1877, there was no specificity around infant death, and this was, possibly, because infants were viewed as a "biological object" and not a person in the same sense that adults were.[12]

The cultural historian Phillipe Ariès postured that in the premodern era, the likelihood of your child dying was so high, that parents had to prepare themselves for the worst by not becoming too attached to a child in infancy.[13] As medical interventions improved, he claimed parents could allow themselves to attach to the hope that their child would survive, and therefore people started to treat children as more of a permanent (within reason) fixture. Whilst it may be true these parents tried to protect themselves, it doesn't remove the grief that will have existed for them, regardless of age. Knowing a child may die in infancy wouldn't have stopped the release of the powerful hormones that allow you to bond with that child.

I have often heard people talk of this increased mortality in history and how parents "just got on with it then." Did they? According to whom? Yes, children were a lot more likely to die, but it is a massive assumption to make that those losses weren't significant for their parents. Believe

---

11   https://www.parliament.uk/about/living-heritage/transformingsociety/private-lives/death-dying/dying-and-death/registeringdeath/#:~:text=In%201833%20an%20accurate%20general,what%20would%20be%20expected%20today

12   https://www.researchgate.net/publication/227581305_The_invention_of_infant_mortality

13   https://www.representingchildhood.pitt.edu/pdf/aries.pdf

me, just because you know they are going to die, doesn't make their death any less painful. Just because we have done something a certain way, doesn't make it right. Remember when we used asbestos for buildings and thought smoking was good for a sore throat?

There is no value in taking apart every decision we made when it came to Dexter's life, and one thing we did decide was to not have him live in a clinical environment. We opted for a DNACPR partly for this reason. We made these decisions because no matter what interventions were in place, the outcome would always be the same. He was always going to die. Therefore, as we had no idea of what kind of pain he might be experiencing, we decided we wouldn't prolong his life with aggressive intervention, as we were the only beneficiaries. I will once again emphasise that this was *our* personal decision and not a judgment on anyone who does decide differently. Doing what is right for you and your family is the most important thing and that won't always be the same decision as for someone else in a similar position.

I maintain that I have few regrets from Dexter's life. However, since he died, I have often said that I wished we hadn't decided so adamantly on no intervention to keep him here longer. Not only so that we got more time, but also, because I have often been made to feel that as he was so young when he died, our loss doesn't hold the same significance as if he of been 4 or 8 or 17.

I am a writer, so language is incredibly important to me. This is why I am sensitive to the inference of language. In songwriting we use this technique a great deal, as literal doesn't always translate artistically, so of course I often notice it more readily. It is the reason that I say I lost a "child," or "my son (or child) died," and I lean away from the term "baby loss" although I have no problem with it being used. I do still say it in certain situations, but I have seen the difference in people's reactions when you say you lost a baby. They are almost dismissive, as though it happens so often that it doesn't really matter. But a child? Now that is a tragedy according to the faces of some people.

Society seems to have instituted a hierarchy of death when it comes to children. It seems to have been decided that there are more significant or painful deaths depending on the circumstances. I have only experienced the death of one living child, and I was informed the day after he was born that he was going to die and then was given an idea of how quickly that would happen. I have no experience of being told my healthy child may die. I don't know what feelings a parent will experience in that. My heart hurts at the mere thought of it. I have spent a lot of time with families who have had this tragic experience, and it is always difficult to listen to the more intimate stories of their diagnosis and subsequent death. I still never, ever compare our losses. All I can know is the shared experience. As they are a member of *The Club* we can then also talk about their experience and feelings openly and honestly.

The one thing that we all agree upon is that child loss is child loss. This is not to say there are no situations that may seem "worse." No one is saying you can't have those thoughts and feelings. We are only human after all. Personally, I feel like there are ways in which children die which must be unacceptably difficult and there are special ways in which those parents should be supported. Ultimately, however, we have landed in the same place, without our child.

Bereaved parents are all in very different places and that is okay. People have varying ideas about how to deal with grief, and yes, even bereaved parents may prescribe to a hierarchy of death. I'm not here to judge that but rather to warn you that, like in any situation, there will always be disagreement. You may well come across bereaved parents who feel strongly that their loss is worse somehow or they may say they don't think someone else's loss is as significant as theirs. Supporting them through their grief is all about allowing them to have these moments. Their space to feel however they want to is crucial in their journey of grief. As I have mentioned before, there are also specialist bereavement groups for specialised types of death, so this may be a good place to direct someone with a very specific need. I have listed some of these in the Resources part of this book.

It is not unusual for bereaved parents to appear angry at other parents that they may see in situations around them. Generally, these sorts of feelings are fleeting and will become less frustrating over time, but it's not hard to understand why someone who has just attended the funeral of their child might get a little upset about someone swearing at their kid at a bus stop. I'm not saying it is fair, but neither is your child dying.

I guess what I am saying here is please, be patient with us. Sometimes the decisions we make are going to be made from a place of anger, but don't mistake that for being irrational. The way that we see the world has changed.

When your child dies, you are gifted something incredible and that is perspective. It changes the way that you view everything in life. Think of it like an Instagram filter over everything we do, that changes fundamentally how we see and react to the world around us. It might not feel real to you, but it is visceral to us. So, there may be times when we push back on the things you say that you mistake for over-sensitivity. For me, the title of this chapter is one of those times. It makes my blood boil.

I know you don't mean my baby didn't matter. I know you're not trying to make it seem like his loss isn't significant, but when you start any phrase with "at least" my blood pressure will immediately rise, and I will start working out how to ask you why you feel my grief isn't valid. My directness might not be your friend in that moment.

I am at a point in my journey of grief where my passion for changing the narrative means that I am more than willing to make someone uncomfortable in this situation. It's not that I don't care about your level of comfort. I do. That said, I feel more passionately about the comfort of a bereaved mother to be able to tell you her son's name is the same as your son's name. Or a bereaved father who wants to have his daughter's name tattooed on his arm without awkward looks and head shaking. I care more about their level of comfort because the rest of the world doesn't.

What you say matters. We will remember it far longer than you will. Remember that if you say, "At least he was just a baby," you'd better be able to tell me the age it would have started to matter that he died.

WISDOM NUGGETS

❖ Again, please don't start any sentence with "at least." It minimises and invalidates our _ grief.

❖ Please understand that there is no scenario in our minds that our child dying is fair. No parent should have this happen, and this phrase can make us feel as though we should be grateful for some part of their death.

❖ Understand that bereaved parents may have differing opinions on subjects and that is OK, but that is for them to choose.

❖ Accept that sometimes we may take things the "wrong way" so please be patient with US.

❖ Recognise that if we do talk about our child, we may well get upset but that isn't because we are talking about them, but rather that they have died.

CHAPTER SIX

"They Are In A Better Place."

"Faith doesn't erase grief."

Kate J Meyer

It is a huge assumption to make that someone has faith, or they may take comfort from your beliefs about an afterlife. I know that many times I have envied those with faith. They can seem better at accepting that there is some plan that accounts for their loss and that there may also be a chance that they will one day be reunited with their loved one, but the simple reality is that their faith doesn't make their loss any less devastating.

I am agnostic. Yes, I'm one of those people not willing to commit to non-belief, rather I want to leave the door open lest I miss out, but I find it hard to believe that any grand plan should involve the death of children. The world we live in doesn't help that feeling either. Children are often the collateral damage to the wants of powerful men and that makes it even harder to believe that someone powerful and all-knowing is ultimately watching out for them.

It seemed disingenuous to talk about faith through my own experience which is mostly based on a few years in a Baptist church in my hometown (incidentally where I discovered I could sing), so it made for a good opportunity to sit down with a dear friend.

I met Samailah through another dear friend.

Samailah is a force of nature. She takes space with a magnetic smile, and she is taller than average. To be fair I'm 5 foot 2 most people don't struggle to tower over me. Within all of this, she makes you constantly feel as though she has her arms wrapped fully around you. Her huge brown eyes are pools of pride for both her blood family and her chosen family and once you are in her circle, your place is cemented in her life. I will never not know a world without Samailah in it, thank goodness. She is political and questioning and will hold you to account if she feels it necessary. She also lives with the most incredible heartache.

Very early into our friendship, she told me about Ribqah.

After the second trimester of pregnancy, Samailah felt strange. That word has such a different meaning for bereaved parents. It goes from being quite a benign piece of language to the only possible way to describe your feelings in some of the worst moments of your life. There wasn't any one thing, but more a sense that something felt "off."

Becoming a parent, especially for the first time, is utterly terrifying. We can say that it's the most natural thing in the world, but the reality is, the whole process is fraught with danger. From development in the womb to birth, to the risks of everyday life, no part of being a parent is easy, but the rewards are magical. So we continue ahead, told by everyone around us that everything will be fine. Somewhere along the way, for many people, they forget to trust their instincts. There is a saying in the medical world; when you hear hoof beats, think of horses, not zebras, (Dr Theodore Woodward) and in essence, it makes sense. In the world that I'm in, however, there are times that this adage has led to disastrous results.

I believe more times than not, a mother's instinct is correct, and we need to be better at following this.

From April 2024, the NHS in England will institute Martha's Rule,[14] a new set of medical guidelines that essentially encourage medical professionals to listen to parents' concerns more closely, keeping them in the loop of medical decisions, and taking in to account their feelings around their child's care.

---

14   https://www.england.nhs.uk/patient-safety/marthas-rule/

In 2021 13-year-old Martha Mills fell off her bicycle whilst on holiday with her parents. After her admission into the hospital, her condition deteriorated and despite her family's insistence that she be moved to intensive care and that something was wrong, their pleas were ignored and Martha died, unnecessarily, of sepsis. Her mother Merope is incredible and has campaigned hard to have this rule put into place. The price she has paid to know what she knows now, however, is far too great.

It is easy to dismiss a first-time pregnant mother's cries that something is wrong, as we know they have no idea what to expect other than what they have read in books or seen on shows. Many of these books and shows don't talk at length about the sheer number of issues that can arise, however, and for good reason. No one needs to know about everything that can go wrong but it's all the more reason for medical professionals to be reassuring rather than dismissive when concerns are raised. To be clear, *most* professionals do all the right things and even in those situations awful outcomes arise, but if there is a pattern of not acknowledging instinct as a consideration, this needs to change.

Samailah spoke to the midwife at a check-up. The baby wasn't moving in the same way and in her mind, there was a distinct lack of kicks and movement. After a visit to the hospital and being questioned over and over if she was "sure" she just hadn't felt any movements, Samailah eventually got desperate enough to call again and was granted an appointment with the consultant. Having met this doctor before, she felt in good, honest hands. An amniocentesis had been suggested at the midway point in pregnancy and was carried out. During the appointment after the procedure, the consultant admitted that there did seem to be an issue with the lack of movement but didn't have an answer as to why.

When asked to describe how she was feeling, Samailah said that her tummy felt like a washing machine that had stopped working and the washing was just sitting there in the dirty water, moving slowly from side to side every time she moved.

It turns out that gestational lupus is a thing. I had never heard of this before, and certainly had no idea of what it meant. Because of this condition, there are problems with the blood vessels in the placenta, due to inflammation and the formation of blood clots, which means that the flow between mother and baby is compromised (and sometimes completely stopped causing miscarriage or foetal death). This may lead to intra-uterine growth retardation, meaning baby is under-nourished and born small and perhaps under-developed. It may also cause other problems including pre-eclampsia. (NB: This was discovered after Ribqah's death).

In short, this meant that her baby wasn't getting the important nutrients needed to develop and thrive. From time to time, the baby was getting a hit of nutrients, and that would account for the sudden movements that Samailah was feeling at 33 weeks pregnant. The doctors felt it was time for a caesarean delivery to give the baby the best possible chance.

Samailah is the only girl alongside three brothers from a loving, Muslim family of five. She describes her father as a liberal Muslim, a description she also uses for herself, whilst her mother is more orthodox opting for daily prayer and wearing of the hijab, a practice Samailah does not regularly partake in.

For Samailah her Muslim faith is hers alone, her life is what she chooses, as her god is the only one she has to answer to. Islam remains a part of her life because of this outlook and allows her some of the most beautiful parts of this organised religion that I envy. Her respect for how anyone chooses to practise their faith is loving and kind, as we imagine faith should enable us all to be.

Before there appeared to be any issues in Samailah's pregnancy, her mother and uncle had decided to go to Hajj. Hajj, in Islam, is the pilgrimage to the holy city of Mecca in Saudi Arabia. According to the practices of Islam, it is number five of the Five Pillars of Islam that all Muslims must make at some point in their life if they can afford the trip. It was an exciting expedition for her mother and although it was over the time of the pregnancy, because of their faith, both Samailah and her mother felt that at least if anything did go wrong, she would be as close to Allah as she could be so that she could pray directly to him for his strength and love. To make sure they could adhere to their pilgrimage as strictly as possible, Samailah made the decision not to tell her mum about the impending delivery. It felt like the right decision at the time.

The remaining family gathered, frightened, around Samailah, offering her the kind of strength that only the closest people in your life can give you, and whilst they were riddled with their own fears, they gave in to all of her last-minute demands, including a pizza, chips, and chicken nugget feast on the way home from the hospital before nil by mouth had to be adhered to.

Before the surgery, Samailah called her mother and confessed that she was about to go into surgery and the baby would soon be here. Through tears, her mother told her that yesterday, in a store she had visited, she had bought a pink blanket. She saw this blanket and knew she just had to buy it, but most importantly, it had to be pink. They cried together and her mother promised to pray as Samailah was wheeled into theatre.

Her father came into the theatre with her and suddenly, her modesty kicked in and she tried to cover her legs, embarrassed that her dad would see them. He rolled his eyes and pointed out he had changed her dirty nappies as a baby, so this was nothing. After this exchange, and an epidural, things happened quickly, and her beautiful, but silent daughter, Ribqah, was born.

Ribqah is an Arabic equivalent to the English name, Rebecca. It means "wife of Isaac" and a 'knotted cord' and holds sacred and positive qualities for a child with the name.

After a quick look at the baby, with big open eyes and a face reminiscent of Samailah's grandmother, she was taken to be looked over and Samailah was wheeled into recovery, quickly texting everyone that the baby was here, and she was a girl—just a normal text like any other, "make sure you get bread with the shopping" that kind of thing.

Weighing in at only 3lbs, it became apparent that Ribqah needed a little extra care so she was moved to the special care baby unit. There is no good way to be taken to the SCBU. It is only used for cases where babies need extra care, and the medical staff on these wards deal with these exceptional little ones daily, so it truly is the best place for your baby to be if they are struggling. That doesn't mean they aren't a stressful, worrying place to find yourself.

Samailah's mother returned from Saudi Arabia on Christmas day, the family and some chosen friends came together and visited with traditional gifts and food and a celebration was underway for the new baby, but there was an air of concern. Daily, Samailah's father would sit with Ribqah in special care, shaking his head in disbelief that this was even happening, concern growing for his beautiful granddaughter and his only beloved daughter.

On December 29, Samailah took Ribqah home. She was now the heaviest baby on the ward, despite still being just under 4lbs, and she was putting on weight. A frantic trip to Babies R Us and a few thousand pounds later, the house was ready for the new arrival, and Samailah and Ribqah arrived home on December 31.

The first baby in the family is often a big deal, not the least in a Muslim family and community, and Ribqah's arrival was no exception. The house looked like a florist shop, and person after person arrived to see the newest addition and coo at the wonder of life and gift from Allah.

On January 7, Samailah was bone tired. There is nothing quite like the tiredness of having a newborn baby, no matter how much you try to rest. Adhering to the age-old advice of sleep when the baby is sleeping, she and Ribqah went down for a nap. A few hours passed, she woke and looked at her beautiful daughter sleeping. She touched her and noticed the cold. Moving her hand to Ribqah's head, her heart screamed, "NO!" She knew. The baby wasn't breathing and Samailah picked her up and put her on her chest begging her to take a breath. She called her dad's number and announced, "My baby is not breathing" and swiftly hung up. Then she called 999. In what seemed like seconds, her father arrived, and the 999 operator was talking Samailah through infant resuscitation. Her dad sat there shaking his head, looking at her, knowing full well this was all futile.

Her brother stepped into the ambulance with Ribqah and Samailah went in the car with her dad, who at one point told her she had to stop screaming so he could drive. Samailah had heard gurgles when listening for Ribqah's breathing and felt convinced that she had still in fact been breathing when the ambulance arrived.

When she arrived at the hospital, everything seemed horribly quiet. No one would look at her. Out of the corner of her eye, she saw her eldest brother, holding her precious daughter to his chest. She knew she was gone.

I have talked of the guilt and shame that comes with the death of your child, and in a discussion with someone at the hospital, Samailah kept saying the words, "It's my fault." To me, this seems a natural reaction. This whole scenario goes entirely against what we feel are our responsibilities as parents. Of course, she thought it was her fault. Unfortunately, in Samailah's case, her words were taken quite literally, and the police were instructed to interview her to investigate suspicious death. (I will go over the reasons for this in Part 2).

Eventually, Ribqah's death was ruled a "cot death," a misunderstood and distressing diagnosis of which we still know very little. The NHS describes it as "the sudden unexpected and unexplained death of an apparently healthy baby." Around 180 babies will die in the UK from SIDS (sudden infant death syndrome) annually, and although research efforts have offered many more answers over the years sadly, there is still no cure. We do know however that babies who are born with low birth weights are 5 times more likely to die of SIDS, but most importantly, we know that whilst there are some preventable risk factors, no one is to blame.

In the Muslim culture, when a death like this occurs the community assembles. To the outsider, it can look like the most incredible support mechanism, a reminder that no one will truly be alone in this. In the midst of this, as a bereaved mother, Samailah was broken and more alone than she had ever felt in her life. In her mind, she had always thought, when things were bad, she would take things 6 months at a time. So she sat and waited for it to be July for everything to be okay again, knowing in her heart that nothing would ever be okay at any point from now on. Meanwhile, food flowers and gifts were being delivered along with more visits and more people in the house to offer their condolences.

As with any culture, the immediate coming together of people is usually quick and large and the Muslim culture is no different in this way. After a while though, this can be exhausting. Grief is already exhausting, other people coming and going just add to this. Despite words from a friend to let Samailah rest, people just kept coming.

In the midst of what was her most acute grief, Samailah found herself cursing her god. Why would he do this to me? Why would he take an innocent baby? Has this happened because I am a bad Muslim? Did I deserve this because I didn't pray enough? She asked a devout relative why Allah would do this to her. This particular relative is a very traditional Muslim man and is someone who never looks women outside his family in the eye, as is dictated in his faith, as a mark of respect. Samailah begged him for an answer to why Allah would do this. He touched her head, looked her in the eye and said, "Allah will give you patience." Tears came to his eyes, he turned his head and walked away. To even the most devout, it can be difficult to fathom such loss, and he knew nothing he said would change how she felt or make any of this better.

In any faith we are taught that to behave well will bring us good, and to behave badly will bring us punishment. What kind of behaviour would warrant taking our child? That is the question that Samailah kept asking herself. Around her, people offered reasoning and words of support they felt related to both her loss and her faith. Perhaps most difficult was the thing that was said the most frequently. *Ribqah was her ticket to heaven.* Because she had died as a baby, Samailah now had, in essence, a free pass to heaven. No matter what she did it would be forgotten, and she could join Ribqah in heaven, as she was waiting at the door to take her mother's hand and head on into paradise. God will have said to her "go in" and she would say "not without my mother." This is dogma that exists in all of the primary organised religions, though the wording may differ.

As Samailah puts it, however, what could she ever possibly do that would be bad enough for the sacrifice for her place in heaven to be her child? What kind of monster would she have to become?

This is why the idea that death is somehow better than life because it involves a paradise filled with love and light, isn't guaranteed to bring comfort, even amongst people who do hold faith. The fact that faith is so personal means we can't truly know what someone's relationship with their god is in this situation, and it helps no one to assume that it will somehow make this journey any easier. Faith doesn't remove grief. It can help with reconciliation as it may give someone a feeling that their loved one is still near or waiting for them somehow, and these things can be an important part of the healing journey, but it doesn't mean that someone with faith will have an easier ride.

There are certainly some elements of faith that I believe can truly help with coming to terms with loss. The primary one of these is prayer. Some people may call this meditation. As with meditation, prayer is proven to be incredibly good for our well-being and using it along with things like meditation and journaling, through grief, can be enormously valuable. Scientifically, we know it regulates heartbeat, improves sleep, reduces stress and can help boost your immunity, all things that can be areas of trouble whilst grieving.

Another is the belief in "signs" or signals that a loved one is still a part of you somehow. Despite my lack of faith, I still refer to Dexter as our angel and I still believe that he watches over his brother and his other loved ones to make sure they are okay. Of the many, many bereaved families I have gotten to know, this is almost always true for all of them. I think human nature is to believe that there is somehow a way that person will stay on in your life, even if it is in only your mind, because, frankly, the alternative, is just too difficult to live with.

Samailah remains a faithful Muslim and still has these conversations with Allah, and importantly, despite feeling for a long time that she didn't deserve it, she was blessed with a wonderful boy named Aarib. His name means handsome and healthy, both of which he has been blessed with in abundance. Aarib and Samailah are incredibly close, something that is common in rainbow babies (the name for children who come after a loss), and their bond is wonderfully special. They share their Muslim faith as part of that relationship. When Aarib was born, Samailah went about reciting all of the special prayers of protection in the four corners of his cot every night before he went to sleep. The Arabic language remains a great source of comfort for Samailah, and Aarib has shown an incredible talent for it now that he has taken to learning it as part of his journey of faith too.

WISDOM NUGGETS

❖ If you know these parents to be of faith, try to adhere to the practices that they have talked of. This can be things like referring to heaven or using the word angel. Follow their lead but most importantly listen to the language they use and don't assume it is rooted in an organised faith.

❖ If a family is spiritual, find things within their faith that may offer some comfort. When Samailah had a family member lose her father, she sat with her gently reading from the Quran, mostly to help her family member see she was not alone in her grief.

❖ Try not to instil your own beliefs, or disbeliefs, on families. Whilst you may not think angels are real, this thought could be the only thing this parent is clinging on to at this point. It's not about rationality, it's about comfort at the beginning and finding it in any way that you can. Over time, they may not use the same language, so continue to listen.

❖ If a parent is devout, be sure to respect this, despite your own belief system. You do not have to partake in anything that you don't feel comfortable doing, but if you can join a parent in prayer or meditation, you may also find that a source of comfort.

❖ If you can encourage them to, try to get them to be still, and take some quiet moments of reflection. Some people may do this already, but other parents may be going all out to change the world in their child's name. It may feel like a compulsion for them at this point. By all means, encourage this, but also encourage them to breathe and take time to just be. In some cases, putting all their energy into fundraising can be a person's way of not facing the truth, try to be mindful of whether that is what you are seeing.

❖ Guided meditation can be a helpful way to take time, especially in the acute phases of grief, being alone in your head can be a little too much, as can trying to get to sleep. I have provided links to valuable guided meditation channels that may help in the Resources section.

CHAPTER SEVEN

Something About Time Blah Blah Blah

"It has been said that time heals all wounds. I don't agree. The wounds remain. The mind, protecting its sanity, covers them with some scar tissue and the pain lessens, but it is never gone."

Rose Kennedy.

For some reason, there is this strange belief that the passing of time makes grief better.

As my friend Virna says, after her beloved son Jordan died, all time does is move our child even further away from us. Of course, the movement of time can make feelings less visceral, but it doesn't remove them, or the physical manifestations that can accompany grief. In an instant, you can be transported to a place where you can feel like you did in the moment of their death. Nothing can prepare you for it and nothing can truly explain why it works like that, but it does. It can be a smell, a sound, or a thought.

The olfactory sense is said to be one of the most powerful at evoking emotional response. Chris insisted I use only natural products whilst I was pregnant with the boys, so the smell takes me right back to my pregnancies. Just the other day I was in a Lush store and covered my hands in "Dream Cream" and all of a sudden I was back in my pregnancy with Dexter like it was yesterday. (Other aromatic high street brands are available).

Again, it's important to remember that even in time, our grief doesn't subside, it just becomes something that we learn to live around. It's not that the pain lessens but that we are more easily distracted by the things that life brings our way. In those first few days, weeks and months, putting one foot in front of the other is our priority, along with the practicalities that death brings; funerals and the like. Then people, and things, return to the place they were before, but a bereaved parent cannot. Their lives are forever changed, and they are left with a reality that reminds them daily that they will never be who they were before. It's the ultimate re-set, rebranding you like Madonna did pretty much weekly during the 1980's.

Then the expectation is that we will just go back as we were before this darkness came. That somehow, we can pick up and go from where we were before we thought our life would imminently be full of nappies and sleepless nights or ballet shoes and football boots. Our environment is probably still full of our child's things, the pieces of them that existed in our day-to-day lives. So, whilst the world moves back to normality, we are constantly reminded of their absence by our hearts, and our homes.

That is not to say that time doesn't help at all with some of the more visceral ways that grief lives in our lives now. The acute symptoms like finding no pleasure in anything, insomnia, and passiveness, these things can lift over time so in that way it is true. The issue is that it seems to come with an expectation that as long as time marches on, our grief will march with it like an obedient soldier. Eventually, you think, we won't feel the loss so greatly, given time. That simply isn't true. The acute feelings will almost certainly come screaming back without warning, but it may feel like the time between isn't just as frequent. That doesn't mean when we least expect it, it won't glide into the room, ball gown on, dance card ready to be filled. (I am currently obsessed with period dramas on Netflix).

Time doesn't guarantee that we won't ever feel this acute grief again, but we can learn to anticipate when we think things may be a little more difficult.

In the year that Dexter would have turned 16, it never occurred to me that it would feel like one of the worst years since he died. The year he turned 4 was hard because he would have started school and when he would have been 10, double figures hurt, and then when he would have turned 13, knowing he would never become a teenager was awful. 16 however was a whole other ball game.

For teenagers, it can be such a big age. So much is made of this illustrious time. It is the becoming of a man, the time a teenage boy often starts to find himself and learn what he is about. It is the final year in high school in the UK, a pivotal time when one will start making decisions about what they will do with the rest of their lives. They have lived long enough and experienced enough to begin to know who they are as a human being. They start to develop a sense of values, often shaped by their parent's values, and they start to see the person they can possibly be.

Knowing Dexter would never turn 16 came with the stark reminder that we would never know these things. What would he believe in? Who would he be? This birthday was one of the hardest yet. Not least because we were watching his brother, at 15, start to have some of these realisations about his own life. As we watch his brother grow, we are reminded of the other part of us who will never grow old. Time will never remove that.

The other thing about time is that it moves differently for everyone.

Some people may experience *complicated* grief or be "frozen" in their journey. In these situations, it may be that they have not had any opportunity since their loss to come to any sort of reconciliation with their grief or they may have put it to the back of their mind in a bid to "get on with life" as expected by others. They may simply be in denial, meaning that the feelings still feel acute. Time, in these situations, can feel like a punishment. If we don't acknowledge feelings, we can't begin to accept them. If someone is living in this state, no amount of time will help.

The other part of the idea that time heals all wounds is wondering what you mean by "heal?" Do you mean that someone will be the same as they were before their child died? That isn't an achievable state of healing because it relies on the idea that your loss was not profoundly life-changing. When a person presents with a treatable physical injury, we don't treat it with "time." We treat it with the medicine we know that works, and therapies that will help in recovery, like physiotherapy.

Again, this imaginary time frame is based on a set of assumptions that the loss of a child will navigate the set roadmap that we have decided that grief follows. No sat nav in existence will help a parent on this journey. There is no google maps for this.

What we need to do is acknowledge that this is an unending situation. No number of tears or anger, no passing of days, will make it any easier or make it go away. So as a bereaved parent, we have to learn to live in a world where it is a core part of who we are now. We need you to allow us as parents to take as long as we need and continue to acknowledge our child existed.

No matter how long it has been, you can't know what element of their child's death is infiltrating their thoughts at any given time. Just because it may seem like a long amount of time for you, doesn't mean there isn't something else playing a part that is making this particular time more difficult.

Bereaved parents may also find particular times of the year difficult. These may be obvious like Christmas or Mother's or Father's day, but they can also be days that you would never have considered like the first or last day of school or other living children's birthdays. Sometimes other celebrations can leave us missing those moments for our own child, and this may seem completely unreasonable to anyone who hasn't lost a child but very real to those of us who have.

There are things that we know do help but sometimes we can struggle to access them. Counselling is rarely readily available for a bereaved parent, with the exception of those who are attached to palliative organisations such as Children's Hospices who may have counselling services available. The system in the UK is stretched beyond belief and even when you can get referred, access is usually only available for 6-8 weeks. Given that around 63% of child deaths happen outside of palliative organisations in the UK, that is a lot of people trying to access help.

Sadly, after speaking with a great number of bereaved parents, it appears that many of them have been immediately offered anti-depressants. I will say this loudly for people in the back; grief and depression are not the same thing. That is not to diminish one over the other or to say that you can't have both, even at the same time. Treating people with drugs that are designed to stabilise your emotions, can remove the ability to reconcile or even acknowledge the feelings of grief. I will say one thing for certain from experience. *You cannot run from grief.* For anyone, and especially for a bereaved parent, it will catch up with you in the end and it will manifest in the most damaging of ways if you don't learn to give it the space it requires to take residence in your life. Grief lives in you now. It is a part of your everyday existence. How big or small a part it takes is determined by how you navigate around it. If you need medication to get through, by all means, you should take it. This is not to say it is never appropriate. For some people, it may be the only way they can get through. Parents need to do what works best for their situation. My point is that it shouldn't be an automatic medical intervention.

The expectation that time somehow makes us okay shows itself to me on an annual basis in the lead-up to Dexter's birthday and anniversary. As a general rule, I will make a social media post stating that for the next few weeks, I may be a little distant, sad or sensitive, as I find the time of year incredibly difficult. I have never shared this without feeling a sense of eye-rolling amongst some people on my platforms. I can tell it from the people who don't acknowledge my post at all, and sadly this can often be from people I would have considered quite close. I don't expect people to message or comment or make any kind of sweeping gesture (that's not entirely true, I kinda do want that), but just some small thing that shows me that they recognise that it might be a tough time and that I am not unreasonable for still struggling all these years down the line. I say quite openly these days that if you don't at least acknowledge what I have said, then I do not consider you a part of my close circle. I am not messing around here. You don't have to say anything, but if you know me, you know how important it is that you acknowledge Dexter's life.

As I mentioned in Chapter 5, I still find it quite astonishing that people make the point that in the past parents just "got on with these things and accepted them." Again I question, how anyone knows that. 25-30 years ago, we didn't talk about menopause, suicide or eating disorders. Now, thanks to the work of people affected by these things, who were willing to put their thoughts and feelings out there, they are being addressed by society and we are recognising the effects felt by people because of them. I said it before, I'll say it again. Just because we have always done something a certain way, doesn't mean we have been doing it correctly.

I have lost count of the number of times that I have spoken about Dexter, and someone has told me about a relative who experienced child loss a long time ago and they were told to just "move on" and never speak of it again. Just because that is how it was dealt with, doesn't mean that those parents still don't grieve for that child. "It was a long time ago" or it "happened all the time back then" aren't suitable responses here.

Their grief still lives within them. Many of them will have built a fortress around it, unwilling to grant entry until someone willing to listen appears, encouraging them to lower the drawbridge and finally talk about their loss. Protecting themselves has become a core part of who they are, and it is only when someone offers them safety by way of opening up the conversation, that they may feel able to share one of the most difficult experiences they have endured. It breaks my heart that this is often the first time, in a long time, that they may have spoken about their loss.

We really need to do better.

WISDOM NUGGETS

❖ Don't say "Time will help." It won't. Nothing will. It will be a long time until it doesn't hurt so acutely.

❖ Understand people are not always ready for counselling. It can have incredible benefits but only when someone is ready.

❖ Even when a lot of time has passed in your mind, recognise that for us, it can often feel like yesterday. We are not "wallowing" or "bringing it up again", we are grieving. That never stops for us.

❖ When you see us mention our child on social media posts, a simple "like" or love heart is enough for us to see that you acknowledge our emotions at that time. Gestures don't have to be big, but they do need to exist.

CHAPTER EIGHT

"You Still Have Your Other Children."

"Before you tell a grieving parent to be grateful for the children they have, think about which one of yours you could live without."

Unknown.

As a parent, you enter into a virtual contract with a set of responsibilities to the child you have brought into the world. At the very top of the list is to keep that child safe. When your child dies, the sense of failure in not being able to do this important job can be all-consuming. Regardless of how your child died, them not being alive means in your head that you have let them down; you've failed. After this, if you already have other children, not only do you still have to parent them but the fear of what may happen to them can become something that you can find very difficult to be rational about. You also quickly realise that no one, not any other child, can replace the one who died or alleviate the pain.

As mentioned earlier, losing a child means joining *The Club* that no one wants to join, and the privilege in that is that you can find yourself surrounded by other people who have that shared understanding and some of them along the way can become very good friends. Friends who you don't have to protect or explain yourself to. People you can talk about anything with and know that they have probably had some of the same thoughts as you.

From this club, into my life, and my heart, came Nicola Graham.

Nicola is a bundle of curly brunette energy. She has a 100-watt smile and one of the biggest hearts of anyone I know. Her presence makes you feel warm and calm, and you just know by being around her that everything is going to be alright. I don't know if she was always this way, but I know that she is shaped in part by a blonde-haired ray of sunshine named Reuben.

In August 2012, Nicola, her husband Mike and two boys, Isaac and Reuben set off to Devon on a family holiday. Reuben had been a little poorly for a few of the previous weeks before the holiday, but he kept rallying and Nicola, and the several doctors they had seen, thought there wasn't really anything to worry about. Off they set to spend time together on the beach, making memories of a happy, sunny childhood.

During the holiday, Reuben fell and when he became pale and distressed, the family took him to the local A&E, unbeknownst to them that this was the beginning of the worst 7 days of their lives.

Reuben didn't respond to some of the tests and was referred for a CT scan. When the results came back, Nicola and Mike were told that Reuben had a very large mass on his brain, which the doctors suspected was a tumour. There was a rush to get him into surgery and he was quickly transferred to a larger hospital where plans were made for after the initial surgery. Despite their best efforts and Reuben fighting hard, his body started to shut down and he was moved into the paediatric intensive care unit to give his body time to rest and recover. Sadly, this never happened and Reuben died, in Nicola's arms on Tuesday, August 21, 2012, at the tender age of 23 months.

Reuben had an atypical teratoid rhabdoid tumour (ATRT), a very rare and aggressive form of a cancerous tumour.[15] So rare in fact that at the time of writing only 4 to 5 children in the UK will be diagnosed with this type of tumour in the next 12 months. The number of patients who survive for 5 years is approximately 32%. It usually affects children under 3 and is very hard to diagnose as its symptoms are not dissimilar to just regular childhood ailments like vomiting, fever or falling down.

---

15   https://braintumourresearch.org/pages/types-of-brain-tumours-atypical-teratoid-rhabdoid-tumour-at-rt

ATRTs are embryonal tumours, which means they develop from stem cells that help the embryo form in the womb, but they have unfortunately remained active in the brain after birth. When these stem cells fail to stop dividing and developing after the child is born, they can form a cancerous tumour.

Two days after Reuben died, even before his funeral, Nicola started Reuben's Retreat, a charity that would ensure that Reuben's short, but precious life, wasn't in vain. Nicola fiercely believes that we have the ability to leave the world a better place than we found it. She wanted this charity to be Reuben's legacy to reinforce her belief that each life, however brief, forever changes the world.

Set in beautiful countryside in the northwest of England, Reuben's Retreat is a beacon of light for families of children with complex needs and bereaved families. It is a space where they can come and create memories or simply relax and recharge. They also provide ongoing support for bereaved families by way of support groups and holistic activities. Their goal is to walk "side by side" with families, ensuring they never feel alone wherever they may be on their journey. It is truly the most wondrous place full of love and magical human beings who give so much care to the people they help.

The thing that makes Nicola one of my heroes is that she has turned her pain into purpose. This is why I feel such a kinship with her. Her passion for helping people is evident from the moment you meet her, so it felt right to include her, and Reuben in this book.

Following Reuben's death, Nicola and Mike also had another thing to consider, their surviving child, Isaac. At just 4 years old when Reuben died, Isaac was an age where he didn't necessarily have a great understanding of what was happening, but he was suddenly thrown into a world of deep sadness, especially for his parents who were broken by the loss of their youngest son.

As I have said before, many parents will go into a kind of *work* mode after the death of their child and Nicola was no exception. Her passion to bring Reuben's Retreat to the place it is now became her sole purpose outside of her family. However, there were people along the way who couldn't understand this compulsion at all. In fact, they outwardly criticised her focus. Nicola always says there is no room for negativity as she explains that losing Reuben was enough negativity to last a lifetime. Saying that, comments can still sting.

Along her journey, Nicola learned from a colleague of a comment that took her breath away. Someone known to a staff member at a local, supportive business had been following Nicola's progress on Reuben's charity and openly disapproved of her focus. "What she seems to forget is she's got another son. And maybe she should be concentrating on him."

For context, this comment was made within the first year of Nicola's loss. That first year is one of acute shock and sadness. Not much can seem worth anything during this time other than what your brain can manage to focus on to get through each day. Here we are all these years later and Nicola vividly remembers this comment being made like it was yesterday.

On reflection, whilst the comment was hurtful, it also made her question herself as a parent. Later, she would understand that losing a child in those early weeks, months and years would be and could be, all-consuming.

This is Nicola in her own words.

'It made me incredibly sad because what a lot of people won't necessarily know is that a lot of parents, and certainly a lot of mothers, can lose themselves in grief for a long time. The loss is so massive, and just so insurmountable that you can't think about anything else. It's almost like you carry an untreated gunshot wound. You know it's there, there's no alleviating and no escaping the pain of it. Especially in those early days. It's nonstop. And so, this comment took me to this incredible place of guilt, because I was already battling with losing Isaac in a way because I wasn't the Mum for him that I felt I could have or should have been, because of the loss and grief and trauma of it all. There isn't any easy way to lose a child. I just remember feeling incredibly guilty and it was so unkind to say as well.'

Alongside perspective, bereaved parents also develop resilience, but this can take time to set in. It almost acts as a way that we can enter back into the real world without falling apart every time we think about what has happened. We have to be able to see that life isn't always going to be as dark as it feels at this moment in time and perspective helps us do this. Nicola says that in going out and making Reuben's charity come to life, she had to build up for it, she had to put that face on and tell the world about Rueben and her grief in order to make it happen, so over time that became how she was. In her words, she would "go to the opening of an envelope" if it was for Reuben's Retreat to be successful, in her private life, things were very different.

Nicola's family is a very social one. When you meet them, you can still sense the charisma that all of them have. After Reuben's death, the family and social things became difficult. Nicola, like many bereaved Mothers, lost confidence in herself as a Mum, but also as a person. Being around people who knew her vulnerability became very hard and for a while she found herself finding reasons not to do social things. It reiterates the notion that losing a child truly tears away your confidence as a human being. Building that confidence back up takes time and energy and at this point, all Nicola's energy was going into setting up Reuben's Retreat and helping her family navigate their way through their terrible loss.

The loss for Isaac of his little brother was devastating. For many their sibling relationship is one of camaraderie, sometimes alongside friction of course, but it usually comes with a profound bond. Your sibling is often your first-ever best friend. All of a sudden, Reuben wasn't here, and Isaac's parents were upset and there was nothing he could do to make it better.

Nicola often says, "If you could lose your brother at a good age, approaching 5 was a good age for Isaac as he knew Reuben well enough and for long enough to remember him, whilst not quite understanding that death was permanent. Therefore, losing Reuben was something he grew up with and learned to live with. I am not saying he didn't grieve or cry and miss him, there was lots of that too. But I also thought for a good 12-18 months later, Reuben could come back to our lives 'tomorrow' and Isaac would just casually say 'Where have you been?' I feel fortunate that he didn't quite grasp the 'forever' of loss."

Again, the sense of wanting to protect your children at all costs plays on your mind. In this case, Nicola was dealing with her own acute grief but also watching her surviving child be heartbroken, with his young mind desperately trying to understand what had happened to his brother. Children also fear the same thing happening to you, and when you have been through a situation where your child is essentially fine one day and then 7 days later, they are gone, how do you truly put your other child's mind at ease when your own fear at this time is visceral? You would give your life to make sure that this child stays okay, but again, it is out of your control. As the Clergyman Sydney Smith said in the 1800's "the life of a parent is the life of a gambler."

The language we use around siblings about their loss is very important. We often say in the bereavement world that children are much better at grief than we are. Kids say what they think. They rarely sugar-coat things but over time, we tend to instil in them in that British politeness and they edit more as they are taught to. As an Australian, I have maintained a sense of directness that I am sure can often seem confrontational, but actually, I just think it's easier and quicker to get to the point! So, I find this frankness in children around death to be healthy and refreshing. Obviously, there are parts of the process that may well be too traumatic for a young brain to reconcile, but when it comes to talking about death with children, the more honest you are, the better.

The best example of this are the words we use around death. Telling a sibling that their brother or sister has "gone to sleep" can feel like a gentle way of saying they have died. However, children don't always understand this metaphor, so suddenly, sleep becomes terrifying because they think they might not ever wake up. As a family, deciding what and how you will tell siblings is an important consideration, so everyone must be on the same page. If you haven't recognised the words being used, this is a good time the ask the question directly.

Children can also find the experience of having lost a sibling to continue to be upsetting and confusing as they get older, which is why support is so important for them. Around the age of 11 or 12 bereaved siblings may have started to have a better understanding of what death actually means, so this can be a difficult time of discovery for them. What they have lost may seem more real for them around this age. This is an important part of why places like Reuben's Retreat, offer sibling support groups.

Being around other bereaved siblings can be helpful for some, giving them a chance to just be kids without having to worry about anything else. Bereaved children may be overly protective of their parents, feeling that they must shield them from more hurt. It is difficult for any child to see their parent in pain, and when this is an ongoing situation like grief, there is often a maturity that sets in for these children. They have to grow up that little bit quicker and learn that the world is not all unicorns and rainbows. It can also, however, make them quite incredible human beings. Many of the bereaved siblings I have had the privilege to work with have grown through their grief to move into careers involving care or research. Many of them have a patience and maturity that I don't see in a lot of adults!

Nicola sees her responsibility as Reuben's mummy to keep his memory alive, and Isaac is an important part of doing that. Reuben remains a vital part of the Graham family and the work that is done in his name is transformative for the families they help. The family have a closeness and a mission and rarely a week goes by when I don't see Nicola, Mike and Isaac's faces celebrating and helping in Reuben's memory, and importantly, in the signs that he sends to let them know he is always right beside them. Every time I see the number 23, I think of Reuben and smile.

WISDOM NUGGETS

❖ Make sure that you understand how the family is referring to the child's death and use the same language eg; "died" or "passed away" as opposed to ambiguous phrases like "gone to sleep." The same applies to signs or "where" the family is referring to the child having gone. For some this is heaven, some may refer to them as being an angel. Listen to how they speak of them and regardless of your own beliefs, go along with their language when speaking to siblings.

❖ Offer to take siblings for trips out or activities. This grief is all-consuming for their parents and children can acutely feel like no one is thinking of them. It also reinforces that although they are very sad, it is ok to still enjoy things.

❖ Be open to listening to children talk about memories of their sibling. Just because it makes you uncomfortable doesn't mean you should shut them down. Talking is natural and healthy. So is crying.

❖ Say their sibling's name around them. Tell them your memories of their sibling. When children hear adults openly talk about something, they understand that it is also ok for them to do that.

❖ Offer to do things like washing and cleaning for parents that mean they can spend time with their other children. Encourage them gently to do things together.

CHAPTER NINE

"I Didn't Want To Upset You."

*"Give sorrow words; the grief that does not speak whispers
the o'er-fraught heart and bids its break."*

William Shakespeare.

I can understand why people say this, but it is probably the one that makes me most upset.

You talking about my child isn't reminding me that he died. I will never, ever forget that.

It feels so counterintuitive to think that not speaking about someone who existed will somehow result in us feeling better not worse. Our child's name is beautiful. It is important and when you say it, it reminds us that you also think of them, which helps us feel less alone. It tells us that you remember them and that they are also important to you. That their memory means something to you. That their life did.

When you behave as though they never existed you deny us the ability to share their memories without judgment. Once again, we can feel silenced into not speaking of them to spare your discomfort. For you to feel comfortable, we have to pretend that a fundamental part of our lives never existed. I know that's not really what you want.

No one is asking you to talk about them every time you see us. No one is saying that you have to listen to upsetting details of our child's death. In fact, of all the people you know, we are probably more inclined to be thinking about how our grief makes you feel.

Because of our experience, we are often more likely to be the people who reach out quickly to those who experience grief. I know that I make a point to ask people about their losses and acknowledge them, but I also know that this is partly because I feel so overlooked and forgotten by people in my own loss. I know by doing this I have some control over people not being left alone in their grief.

This is not to say that we are not getting better. Especially with social media so heavily at play in our lives now. People are willing to share their losses more than ever. Where we have to be careful here is that we are still taking time to feel grief, not just share it for the acknowledgement on social media. Para-social relationships can be very important, but they aren't the only way that someone should work through their grief.

When, in 2023, Derian House Children's Hospice surveyed families who had used the service, they found that more than eight out of ten families said they felt sad that people no longer use their child's name. Overwhelmingly, families said that they desperately wanted to talk about their late child, but they felt people actively avoided the subject. More than half of the families felt their child had been completely forgotten.

Imagine that. Imagine no one spoke about or acknowledged your child or loved one when they were standing right next to you. Remember a time when someone overlooked or ignored you and how it made you feel. (Cue my entire high school experience.) Now imagine they did that about someone you loved with all of your heart. Your child. Imagine that rather than acknowledge their existence, they just ignored them and pretended that they never existed.

That, in essence, is what you are doing when you choose not to speak about our children. Ignoring their existence. To us, it can feel like they didn't matter, that their life wasn't important.

So why does death, especially the death of a child, make us so uncomfortable? For many, I have heard them say that the idea, even thinking of their own child dying is more than they can bear. Let me tell you a secret about when your child dies. It's more than you can bear.

There are few areas of child death as misunderstood and stigmatised as Stillbirth. Approximately 1 in 250 births in England will result in a stillbirth.[16] In the UK, it is eight babies a day. Eight families who went to bed the night before thinking they were okay, that they were excited about their new family member who would soon arrive. Eight families who then have to go back out into the world and answer all the questions about why they don't have a baby with them, to then oftentimes be ignored, shunned and left to their own devices.

Stillbirth in England is specifically defined as any birth after 24 weeks of completed pregnancy. There are many different reasons that stillbirths happen, many of which may remain unexplained for some families. We know there are certain risk factors, but there is no guarantee that any pregnancy will make it to a healthy delivery.

Perhaps one of the worst elements of stillbirth is the shame that still seems to be attached to it. As I previously mentioned, a sense of guilt can be overwhelming for a bereaved parent, and stillbirth is no exception. However, as most stillborn babies will never meet anyone outside of immediate family, there can be a very real disconnect which can lead to an idea that the child never actually existed in the behaviour that often comes around it. Perhaps the most notable sign of this is that some people decide to completely ignore the birth at all and carry on as though nothing of significance happened.

A few years ago, I had the pleasure of meeting the whirlwind that is Sarah Parsons. Sarah is larger than life. A human ball of emotion, compassion, and love, she is the kind of person who, once she has you, won't let you go. As she says, she never takes no for an answer, and before you know it, you agree to whatever she has initially asked you to do, even though you had gone in with your intentions fully decided in your head! I say that with love, and she is one person you can always rely on to do what she says she will do, and if you do tell her no, be prepared to hear the words "dead babies" because that's how she gets you.

It is important to recognise here, that although they are words that Sar-

---

16   https://www.childbereavementuk.org/death-bereavement-statistics

ah uses, within the charity world, we will often do and say whatever we can to get you to understand the importance of all this work, and we will very often be mercenary about it. So, whilst that is not necessarily the language I would use, I adore Sarah's rough and ready demeanour, and my gosh, does it work!

In 2015 Sarah was glowingly pregnant. After several miscarriages, the diagnosis of polycystic ovarian syndrome and a tilted womb, having a baby felt like an impossibility in her mind. As the centre of her family's universe, aka the oldest child, everyone around her was ecstatic when she told people she was pregnant. Sarah is the kind of person who brings people together. A racing ADHD mind, she is magnetic, and the people surrounding Sarah were happily anticipating her and her partner Mark's little miracle. With nine Godchildren, Sarah being blessed with her own baby was just what everyone around her knew she was made for, so this was going to be amazing.

Throughout her pregnancy, whilst scared and still a little shocked, Sarah documented everything, and I mean everything. Videos of her being sick still get spoken about by family members and as a chronic oversharer, she adored showing every part of this amazing thing as it happened. Little did she know that both her documenting and her propensity for sharing so much would be immensely important later down the line.

As is common in situations like this, Sarah and her baby, which she knew would be a girl, at 35 weeks of pregnancy, there was nothing to indicate a problem with the pregnancy.

Close to the end of the pregnancy, Sarah started to swell. At almost 6 feet tall, Sarah has size 9 feet already, but she was swollen to the point that even her stepdad's size 11, Velcro flip-flops wouldn't fit on her feet. Trying to just get on with things, and preparing for the baby well underway, she had some tests regularly, but nothing was showing as concerning.

After a presentation scan on the Saturday in the birthing suite, the baby was fully engaged and getting ready to enter the world soon enough. Sarah was told it could well happen within the next few days. With baby kicking away under her ribs on a Sunday night, all felt good and on the

Monday morning, a doppler (or a *sound*) scan at Sarah's home was to check for the baby's heart rate, commonly done in labour. The midwife took herself outside to make a phone call.

Sarah overheard the words "There's no foetal heartbeat."

When she heard her say it outside, Sarah's first thought was "Oh My God, she's dead."

But then the doubt set in, and all the questions started flying through her head. "How can she be? She's full-term. I'm due on Wednesday. Wednesday is my official due date."

Sarah rang her mum, who came with her stepdad who drove Mark and her to the hospital. She sat in the back of the car, her Mum holding her, crying tears she thought would never, ever stop. Mark was quiet, shocked. At the hospital, Sarah's sister arrived, and the family waited outside whilst Sarah and Mark were in the scan room when the sonographer uttered those words that changed everything; "We're sorry. There's no heartbeat."

With a scream of anguish, Sarah confirmed to her family, waiting outside, that the baby had died. There would be no daughter, no grandchild, no niece. She was gone.

Once it is established that a baby will not be born living, it is widely accepted that giving birth is the safest way for the mother as a caesarean section is a major abdominal surgery so comes with many risks. Vaginal birth is encouraged and, in most instances, once informed that the pregnancy will not continue, the mother will be offered medication that will induce labour. At this stage, families will be given time to think about how they would like to proceed. Whilst it may seem cruel, giving birth really is the safest option, as a caesarean, as with any big operation, comes with many risks.

At this point for Sarah, the consultant offered her the medication. However, it is important to recognise that for Sarah, this medication offered only the reality that she would have to accept her baby had died. That said, she was convinced that if she took the tablet, she felt she could be killing her baby because, for all she knew, she might be fine once she was born. Any parent is going to fight every thought of the worst in this situation and Sarah was no exception. Sadly though, her baby had already died, and she was going to need to deliver her into the world.

Many hospitals in England have specific and necessary facilities for mothers who will be birthing a child who has already died. Sadly, many hospitals have no such facilities, something we really need to talk about, but that is for another time.

Sarah made her way to the Butterfly Room, a haven where she laboured to bring her daughter into the world. After 36 hours, however, Sarah developed Sepsis and was rushed in for an emergency caesarean. There was a moment there where she almost died, but somehow managed to make it back, despite it being touch and go for a minute.

On her original due date of June 30, all of the sounds in the theatre stopped. The heart monitors, the machines, the lights were all silent and dimmed and at 8.33 pm weighing 8lbs and measuring 59 centimetres long, Maggie Pearl Parsons was born, perfect and sleeping.

None of this was like the magazines said it would be. *Let It Be* played quietly on the radio in the background and Sarah's heart broke into a million pieces.

In the Butterfly Suite, Sarah was visited by a lady called Nadia and given a memory box. As Maggie lay in a "cold cot," Sarah's Dad was flying over from Spain to meet his first grandchild, something Sarah had envisioned a completely different way to what was happening at the moment. Heartbroken, people came to visit. It wasn't until her friend Vicky came; did she realise that she understood the kind of compassion she was going to need to get through this. Vicky fought her way through the nurses at 11.30 pm to make her way into the room to see her best friend from high school and be what was needed in a friend that night. She gently spoke to Maggie, welcoming her to the world and congratulating Sarah on being a Mama, quietly acknowledging what most people had forgotten; that Maggie was now here, and both Vicky and Sarah, knew deep in their hearts that she would change the world, at least their worlds for now anyway. Suffice it to say, that Vicky is Maggie's godmother.

Sarah eventually found out that she suffers from a rare condition called chronic histiocytic intervillositis, an inflammatory placental condition, which left untreated, is associated with very poor pregnancy outcomes. A few years and several failed IVF rounds later, she was sadly unable to have any more children.

Now, working on her charity, Maggie's Stillbirth Legacy, Sarah works tirelessly with organisations to help remove some of the stigma around stillbirth. The charity raises money for cuddle cots and cuddle blankets (I will explain these in Part 2) and is often the first point of contact for many women in hospital who have experienced the painful devastation of a stillborn baby. Full disclosure, I am a very proud Patron of this charity, and I am often in awe of the tenacity and passion Sarah puts into making the experience of stillbirth just that little less lonely for families.

Talking to Sarah about Maggie, one of the things she will tell you she finds most upsetting is the lack of acknowledgement that Maggie existed. She has known people to cross the street to avoid having to talk to her. This is something I have heard from MANY bereaved parents. Sarah is the first to say that Maggie's death absolutely highlighted who was going to remain in her life, versus those friends who would fall to the wayside because they didn't want to deal with the discomfort, or in their words "upset her."

When Maggie was born, as Sarah had been so prolific on social media throughout her pregnancy, she was also active once her daughter had arrived, just now with a different tone. After warning people online, Sarah set up an album of photographs of Maggie and told people that if they didn't want to look at them that was fine, but equally, she was her baby and Sarah was going to have her photographs out in the world.

Sarah gave what is essentially a *content warning*, but it is important to note here that there is a discussion to be had on the issue of sharing photographs like this online. Sarah and I agree that for a parent who has been through a similar experience, these pictures could be very distressing, so at the very least, a warning is required. Equally, photographs are an important way for families to acknowledge the existence of their child and can be an important part of the grieving process. The Victorians practised Memento Mori for a reason after all. Whilst Memento Mori literally means "remember you must die" it became known partly as the practice of photographing the dead or holding keepsakes of a loved one after death and to help us to remember to live each day as a "complete life." It was not unusual for parents to have photographs taken of their deceased child with living siblings, as this would be the only thing they would have that told the world their child had existed.

In England, there is a beautiful organisation called *Remember My Baby* that goes into hospitals to take photographs of stillborn babies or babies who die shortly after birth. They give families meaningful pictures to hold dear and share with those they would like to share with. That is not always something parents will want to do publicly, but it is and should be, a choice that parents can make when they have these pictures. Whilst it might not be something you agree with, this is one of those situations where I say again, with love, it is not about you or your discomfort. It is about parents trying to come to terms with the unthinkable. However, it can be important to gently remind bereaved parents to warn people that they will be sharing pictures, as it should be a personal choice not only to do that but also to see them.

In not wanting to upset a bereaved parent, people will often self-edit what they share with them in the future, and Sarah found that for her, this was one of the most difficult parts moving forward. She went from being the first to know everything, especially pregnancies, to being hidden or unfriended on social media pages as people around her did their best to avoid bringing up anything they thought would lead to upset. It's crucial to remember here, that just because we have lost a child, doesn't mean we can't feel happiness for someone else who has one. Keeping Sarah out of the loop was saying to her not only was she not important anymore but neither was Maggie. At least that's how it felt.

Being a part of other children's lives will always come with a bittersweet taste but more often than not it can make bereaved parents want to be even more a part of your children's lives. After all, we have all the love of a lifetime with nowhere to put it. If you allow us, we can be the most wonderful way to remember to be grateful for your blessings, and we are generally okay with that. We will have moments of course, but mostly, we want to see and hear about those firsts and those special occasions, we just need you to understand that if we get upset, it is because nothing will ever change that our child is gone. You ignoring it might make it feel worse though. Also, there is nothing wrong with tears.

Sarah is keeping Maggie's legacy alive in her work, but also in how she interacts with the people who have allowed her to be a part of their children's lives. She is the life and soul of every room and big smile and even bigger heart draw you in. That is a human that children need to be around. She reminds me daily of what compassion looks like.

WISDOM NUGGETS

❖ Acknowledge our children existed. Say their names and ask about them. If you feel you can, ask about the birth.

❖ Remember that being upset is ok and a perfectly normal part of the process of grieving. There is nothing wrong with being upset and generally, it will be not one thing in isolation that will mean tears. Tears are okay though, and important.

❖ Don't cut us out because you feel like you need to protect us. We can still make decisions and over time, we will sometimes have to make self-preserving decisions but that is okay too. I am always clear with people when they have a baby that it may take me a while to visit but always request many photos and updates. It is up to me to manage situations that may trigger me, so I do.

❖ You are allowed to complain about your children around us. Having kids is hard! Even though this dreadful thing happened to us, we can still acknowledge that it is challenging and exhausting and frequently a thankless task being a parent.

❖ Offer to help with our environment. We will often be returning to a home filled with things for a new-born baby. Whilst we will probably not want to get rid of these things just yet, creating a space where they are not the only thing we see when we get home can be helpful for a little while. We are going to have to deal with those things at some point, but it can be helpful to ask if we would like them to be put away for now.

❖ Memory boxes are a great way to keep things in one place. Try to consider encouraging parents to keep things they might not have thought of keeping. It's not unusual for parents to want to keep most things, including medical equipment such as tubes in this box.

❖ This isn't something that can be fixed. Listening and holding space will go a long way to helping us feel less alone.

❖ Respect our decisions around documenting our child but also remind us that we need to give people around us options. You can gently remind us to offer content warnings on social media or suggest that we create an album on socials to begin with that can be accessed if people want to. Whilst our grief is important to respect, it doesn't mean we shouldn't consider the reaction of others due to their own experiences, and sometimes we may need to be delicately reminded of this.

CHAPTER TEN

"Its Time To Move On."

*"Grief never ends. But it changes. It's a passage, not a place to stay. Grief
is not a sign of weakness nor a lack of faith. It is the price of love."*

Author Unknown

I'm going to be controversial here. That's right, little old non-confrontational, people pleaser me, is going to say something people might not like.

I agree. Hear me out.

I think the language is wrong, along with the intent of many people, but we do need to find a way to move forward, and we need your help to do that.

As I've said, grief is exhausting. If we spent the rest of our lives living in the acute, physical grief that you feel at the very beginning of your loss, there would never, ever be room for anything else. To help, our brain steps in to try to distract us from the grief, one moment at a time. Someone might say something that makes us smile and for a few seconds, we are okay, then someone else might make us laugh and we do it out loud, and then 3 seconds later burst into tears. Laughter is one of the most guilt-provoking parts in all of this. It's crucial but it feels like such a betrayal.

I say this often; when Dexter died, all the light went out in the world.

I thought I would never know joy or see colour again. The idea that I would find something funny or even slightly amusing never entered my mind. The first time I laughed, I then cried and audibly apologised to him, assuring him that he was not forgotten.

I firmly believe that grief and joy can co-exist. In fact, I think it's crucial they do. Without darkness how can we truly know it is light? Without being able to see colour at its most vivid, would the world just look like many shades of grey? That doesn't mean that at that moment I didn't get overwhelmed with guilt. For just a second, I had forgotten that my heart had been smashed to bits.

However, for some people, there is still frustration that their loved one seems to be stuck in their grief. "How hard can it be?" I hear you ask. "Surely they should just be over it by now?" you say to your friends.

Well, there is something I have touched on earlier, but it could do with a little more detail.

Science.

That's right. Solid, undeniable, researched proof that can help us understand just a little bit better why someone may seem like they are struggling to take steps back into the real world.

Thankfully, a lot of people, much smarter than me, although arguably less glamorous, have been studying how the brain and grief co-exist for a very long time. There have been countless studies using everything from MRIs to studying the immune system, to see what is happening to our brain and body when we are bereaved. It is worth looking at the evidence that suggests a grieving brain is actually a learning brain; one that is finding new pathways after the trauma of loss. It is truly fascinating and for a bereaved parent, incredibly validating.

What I want to focus on is why people can struggle with this elusive "moving on" that everyone likes to keep telling us to do. I am going to keep it very simple, mostly for me, but there are neurobiological reasons the bereaved can behave in certain ways.

When after giving birth, a chemical called oxytocin is released that makes us bond with our baby.[17] New dads and non-birthing partners also get this. It is also referred to as the attachment hormone. It is very importantly, the hormone that helps us to forget how much babies cry! Oxytocin is released into the body through things like touch, so adoptive and foster parents can also experience its release into the system. We see this throughout nature, and many studies have been done on animals that we can now translate to human makeup. A study of voles by Julie Sadino and Zoe Donaldson at the University of Boulder, Colorado[18], showed that they mate for life and in their research, they discovered that when they met their soul mate and their attachment was formed, involving oxytocin, their epigenetics changed. That is to say that their genes became different because of this, and the belief is that this may also happen in humans. It is thought that a physical change happens that attaches us biochemically to our person. It also means that we have a physical, stress response that creates cardiovascular, hormonal, and immunological changes when these bonds are broken, especially as a result of the death of a person.

Mary-Frances O'Connor from the University of Arizona talks of these changes as the neurobiological belief that that person will always be in your life.[19] When we are bereaved, two things are happening paradoxically for people though; the memory of that person dying, alongside the neurobiological response that you are still attached to them so unable to reconcile that they are actually, physically, gone. I use the word reconcile a lot when talking about grief, and this illustrates what I mean. Somewhere along the line, our brain must be retrained to understand that person no longer exists in our lives, only in our memory and the time this takes will vary from person to person.[20]

17 https://www.health.harvard.edu/mind-and-mood/oxytocin-the-love-hor-mone#:~:text=Just%20the%20simple%20act%20of,the%20four%20feel%2D-good%20hormones

18 https://www.ncbi.nlm.nih.gov/pmc/articles/PMC6093782/

19 https://news.arizona.edu/employee-news/how-brain-handles-loved-ones-death-qa-mary-frances-oconnor#:~:text=You%20can't%20really%20talk,we%20are%20walking%20around%20with

20 https://www.hmpgloballearningnetwork.com/site/psychbehav/qas/neuroscientif-ic-approach-bereavement-and-prolonged-grief-disorder-dr-mary

So, when you are expecting someone to be further along the line in their grieving, ask yourself how long it took you to master the last new skill you learned. I am currently on a 6-month German streak on Duolingo, and I still can't ask where the nearest toilet is! The brain needs time to learn.

Over time, our brain finds ways to help the days get a little easier. Your brain may help you put things to the back of your mind for a little bit longer each day, enabling you to regain some much-needed strength and energy. However, just because we may not appear to be outwardly grieving, doesn't mean it isn't still there.

I think many times that bereaved parents are victims of their own success. If you look like you're doing okay, people think you are. However, we are often stuck in a purgatory of wanting to still outwardly grieve, whilst knowing that people around us are fed up with our sadness. Let's face it, it is difficult to be around sadness, but it is an inevitable part of life. So whilst it may be hard to be around, ignoring it, does no one any favours.

The public perception of what grieving parents look like is also a little skewed, especially concerning mothers.

In many portrayals of bereaved mothers in the media, there seems to be a focus on anger or mental health issues. Two of the most popular roles that come to mind are the extraordinarily talented Sarah Lancashire in *Happy Valley*, and the multi-talented Kristen Bell in the Netflix hit *The Woman In The House Across The Street From The Girl In The Window*. Both were incredible roles played wonderfully but there was an overwhelming sense of only portraying one side (I'm being general here for brevity). Anger is certainly a part of your child dying. It's infuriating and I want to speak to the manager, but it is not the only thing I feel. I have also, as in the latter show, been troubled by mental health issues since my bereavement, but being unhinged shouldn't be the automatic go-to here either.

As a bereaved parent, you can still be fun and funny, sexy and alluring, charismatic, dynamic, tenacious and talented. (I 100% just listed the things I wrote on my last professional CV by the way). No rule says you have to live your life as the sad story in a Hallmark movie. Although, confession time, I will have definitely watched that movie since my obsession with Hallmark films knows no bounds. What I would really like is more representation of parents who have gone back into the world and made people celebrate life and laugh and smile, please. I look forward to this.

As I mentioned earlier in this book, when your child dies, for many, resilience sets in. Mostly because we do end up seeing and knowing of more children who have died, and we now see the world differently. Crueller perhaps. The gift of perspective may give us a tendency to have a different benchmark for things that other people find very difficult. That doesn't mean that other things in life aren't difficult, of course, they are. Terrible things happen to people all the time. Bereaved parents don't own bad stuff happening. We are not saying we do. Just that we may see the harder stuff differently than others as a result of our experience. However, it is important to remember that some of this is based on your character. If you are a glass-half-full kind of person already, that will possibly be how you use that perspective. If you are the opposite, then it may feel like the hard stuff is harder still. Again, we are all different human beings coming at this with different experiences along the way that will shape how we deal with it.

There is also another consideration here where I want to remove all emotion for a moment. It's what I like to call the economics of grief.

When we don't deal with or allow grief at its most acute stage, it will almost always find a way to come back in detrimental ways in the future. Grief will always find you. It's the bounty hunter of emotions.

Not only are bereaved parents very likely to suffer from poor mental health at some point in their journey, but from meeting and talking with many bereaved parents, I believe undiagnosed post-traumatic stress disorder (PTSD) amongst the bereaved is endemic. Treating PTSD involves complex therapeutic interventions not readily available. (The most common of these treatments is EMDR (eye movement desensitisation and reprocessing)). Even without PTSD, allowing parents to grieve as they need can help prevent many of the issues that can come down the line.

As mentioned in Chapter 7, in many instances, bereaved mothers especially, have told me, that they have been offered anti-depressants. Given we know that the brain has learning to do, doing that whilst muddying the waters with unnecessary medication may only prolong the experience. Make no mistake, I am not against medication. It has an important part to play, when necessary, but it is important to feel feelings, even though they are terrible and hard. If we don't deal with them, they can find themselves manifesting in much more damaging ways.

Having said that, for some parents, medication is exactly what they need to be able to get through the days ahead. Life doesn't stop and for some, there is little choice but to be able to get through in any way possible. To get other children to school or all the other day-to-day errands parents need to get done. Others may simply decide to medicate because they want to. No way is wrong, but it is beneficial to make an informed choice.

If we allow parents time, including appropriate and unpressured, time off from work, we could potentially prevent issues in the future such as depression and anxiety, physical manifestations that can arise from stress like high blood pressure, and in the worst cases, the inability to work at all due to mental or physical health issues. Purely from a socio-economic point of view, it makes more sense to allow parents to properly grieve to save pressure on services in the future.

Sadly, when your child dies, studies have shown that you can even be more likely to die younger yourself[21] along with being more likely to suffer adverse mental health throughout your lifetime. You are also eight times more likely to get divorced.[22] The statistics are already against us, so we need you to help make sure that we are supported in the best possible way.

For some though, going back into the real world isn't an option. I'd

---

21   https://www.sciencedirect.com/science/article/abs/pii/S0277953619305167
22   https://www.ncbi.nlm.nih.gov/pmc/articles/PMC2841012/

say most bereaved parents don't want to ever go back into a world that doesn't have their child in it, but they manage to find a way eventually. That said, there are always going to be people who make that choice to not want to move through. It's a dark place to want to not be living anymore, but I understand. The struggle between wanting to live and not wanting to feel the kind of pain that you feel when your child dies can be too much for some people.

I also think the problem is that when you ask people to move on or assume that they should be better by now, you're asking them to betray the memory of their child and obviously, that's not what you mean, but that's what it can feel like. Those first moments, those first hours and days after your child dies, the idea that you will ever know a normal life again just feels completely and utterly alien to you. Never mind the idea that you might feel genuine human emotion again.

People often use the word brave in the direction of a bereaved parent, and it almost always invokes a sense of frustration. The official definition of brave is to be "ready to face and endure danger or pain and show courage". No one is ready to face this pain. There is no preparation for it, nor do we have any choice in it. Bravery feels like a choice to me. Something you decide to do like running into a fire. I don't want to run into a burning building. I feel like a lot of me would set fire quickly. Is Botox flammable? My point is that we don't want to be here, and we don't even want to keep it together, but for a myriad of reasons, we may have to. That isn't what we generally think of as *brave*, it's just what has to happen.

What is brave though, is taking a step back into the real world when we know that world will probably not allow us to talk about our child often or openly. We valiantly move through a world that would prefer we never mention their name, or that they even existed. In this, we know we are going to have to endure pain, and we have to be courageous to do that. So if you are going to call us brave, please acknowledge that it's for this part.

Most people know that they have to go on. We may have other children or responsibilities. The realities of life don't stop for anyone sadly. For some of us, we have to go on because we need to make sure that the world knows who our child was.

Most people will take the step eventually, they just need the handrails put in place that are built from time, support and understanding.

WISDOM NUGGETS

❖ Understand that there is no timeframe for us and let us know you are aware of that.

❖ Do encourage us to do things in the "normal" world again. We may not be ready when you ask the first time, and we may not even be ready the tenth time you ask, but please don't stop asking. We will get there eventually.

❖ Make sure we rest. As I mentioned, grief is exhausting, and sometimes we might forget that we need to stop and re-energise, especially if we are in fundraising or raising awareness mode.

❖ Recognise that no matter how long it has been, there will always be times for us that are harder than others. Please acknowledge those times, even if you don't understand why, it is significant.

❖ Understand that stepping back into the real world takes courage and remind us that not all of the world in those moments has forgotten our child. Encourage us to talk about how those first days back at work or a social event made us feel. If there have been good feelings, it will reinforce those, making us more likely to feel good about continuing to try. If the experience hasn't been good, it will help us to talk through why.

❖ If you work with someone who is returning after their child has died (or any bereavement really), take a quiet moment with them to acknowledge their loss and encourage other colleagues to do the same. Pretending their child didn't exist and they hadn't just lived through the unthinkable will only serve to make them feel more isolated.

❖ If you see signs that worry you, please talk to us. Ignoring it and thinking we will get through it eventually could be a catastrophic mistake. I never told anyone the first time I felt suicidal, and by the time I mentioned it at all, I don't think people took it seriously because I didn't seem like I was. Make no mistake, there was darkness that I felt I would never escape at times, and it scared me to think that I so seriously didn't want to be in the world anymore. (Thankfully, I haven't felt that way for a little while now, but it does still plague me from time to time). Even if someone says it off the cuff, it doesn't mean it's not a very real consideration for them.

PART TWO

THE PRACTICAL WAYS THAT YOU CAN HELP.

When your child dies, there is a helplessness that is ever present for loved ones. There may be a sense that nothing you do will make anything better. Whilst, indeed, you can't change the situation, there are many different and valuable ways you can help right from the earliest moments. This part of the book is written in a way that can guide you towards the practical and emotional support you can offer.

Part two is written regarding the death of a child that is expected. That is a child who has a diagnosis of a life-limiting or life-threatening illness. This is where my experience lies. In the Resources part of this book, I will outline the different organisations that can help in other scenarios such as road traffic accidents and unexpected death, as they can bring with them some more specific involvement from authorities and care. I have also included a link in the Resources part to the Statutory and Operational Guidance around child death in England.

I have also written this with a Western, Secular or Christian perspective as that is my experience. However, the rituals of Islamic and Jewish rites of death, along with other faiths and cultures, can be very beautiful and I think, are important to know. If you experience a loss within these faiths, I have included links in the Resources part to some websites that outline these rituals and give you a better sense of what may be needed in those scenarios.

Some parts of this may feel uncomfortable to read but knowledge is power, and you will be more able to help if you have a broader understanding of what happens at each part of the process.

Read it as you need to, and once again, look after yourself in it too.

THE FIRST WEEK

There are a few different ways that things can play out here. One is that the child's death is imminent and expected, although one can never truly prepare for it. The family will probably, although not definitely, have had a conversation about how they want the death to be.

They may have asked other family members or friends to come and say goodbye, or they may have decided on just parents in the room. There are no right or wrong answers here. Some parents will choose for the child to die at home, some will have little choice but to stay in the hospital (this will often be the case of children in paediatric special care units for example), and some will be given the option to move to a hospice if there is that support available.

Although a terminal prognosis has been given, a child can still die from what is called an unexpected death and that can make things a little more complicated. In England, if a child's death is expected, as long as they have seen a doctor within the last 2 weeks, there is no need for the police to be involved and also, generally, no need for a post-mortem. If the death is unexpected and happens at home, then the police will need to attend. Even if a child's death was expected at some point, if the child's consultant, the coroner, or other care providers request it, then a post-mortem will be required. This is then compulsory. Sadly I have become an accidental expert at knowing how this all works!

This first 24 hours for the family will be hectic and for most parents, will be done in a haze of acute grief. They may not have discussed their wishes with anyone other than their care team, so it may seem like many things are happening simultaneously.

If a child dies in the hospital, depending on the location, the family may be offered a space dedicated to allowing families time with their loved one, by way of cold blankets or cold cots (depending on the age of the child). These work by cooling the body to slow down the decomposition stage of death, allowing time with their child to come to some kind of terms with what has happened. Some hospitals may have a room where this is possible for a short amount of time, using said blankets or cots. Most hospices have dedicated "cold" rooms, with cooling systems that allow a body to rest for around 2 weeks whilst arrangements are made for the child's funeral.

An important consideration in these moments is the weather. Whilst we are used to the cold and rain in the north of England, which I call home, the last few years have seen "heatwaves" become common in the summer. I use inverted commas there because I am Australian, and it pains me to write the word "heatwave" for temperatures under 30 degrees Celsius!

During these warmer times however, cold blankets, cots and even rooms can struggle to function as they may in cooler weather, so it needs to be a consideration as it will make a difference to how long a child can be laid at rest before their funeral.

These rooms or cots are seen as a stepping stone to a final goodbye; a way to help families begin to reconcile what has happened, knowing that they are going to have to live their lives without their child in it from now on. They can help ease the shock of death, whilst helping their brains understand that their child has indeed gone. Just because a child is lying in one of these rooms, however, doesn't mean that families will visit them. That is a purely individual decision.

When Dexter died, after a few hours, we finally left him with the nurse, in his cot, looking like he was sleeping. We went, broken-hearted, to bed. He was taken to a Sunflower Room and laid there for the days before his funeral. I didn't go in once. I was so frightened that he would look a certain way, and I just wanted that vision in my head of him looking asleep as the beautiful baby he was. Over the years I have said many times that I wish I had gone in to see him, but it wasn't the right decision for me at the time and I have to accept that. It truly is a situation that you can't know until you are in it, but I am very fortunate that I even had that option.

Some families will have their child laid in one of these spaces to allow others to come and say goodbye if they hadn't been able to do that before the death. This again is a very personal decision. A parent may ask you if you would like to see their child, and it is ok for you to say no. How you come to terms with someone's death is your journey to own and putting yourself in a situation that is distressing for you, won't really offer them any more comfort. You need to be honest with yourself about it being the right decision for you. Some people welcome the opportunity and that is fine too.

Several things need to happen in a very short time frame after death, some are procedural, and some are emotional.

Possibly the biggest thing is that people will need to be informed. When I say people, I mean family and friends. This is one of the hardest things a parent has to do.

From a procedural point of view, within five days of death, it needs to be registered at the local registry office. The death will be registered within the county in which the child died, so it must be done at that local county office near either the hospice or the hospital if they died there, or the office closest to their house, if death occurred in the family home. Funerals cannot be held, or even organised sometimes, without this documentation. If you are under hospice or hospital care, you will be given a medical certificate from a doctor stating the time and cause of death. You need this certificate to register the death. You also need money. The registration is free, but the death certificate costs, at the time of writing, £11. You used to need this money in cash, but following COVID you can now pay by card at most council offices.

The family is given the death certificate and a pack that includes relevant information along with a phone number for the Tell Us Once service. This is a service that, in theory, informs several different government departments about the death and starts the process of ceasing payment of benefits and cancellation of passports and the like.

The Tell Us Once service is a relatively new thing. It didn't exist when Dexter died. On the 6-month anniversary of his death we received a rather upsetting letter stating that as we hadn't let a particular government department know he had died, we now owed them £600! Colour me baffled that in registering his death, we had no idea that relevant departments would not be notified. I am so glad this service now exists to make these steps just that little bit less overwhelming.

There are lots of considerations for funerals, including what families like to call them. Some families may prefer it to be referred to as a Celebration of Life. It is not unusual for these celebrations to be colourful affairs, much like a party. There may be balloons and music, and coffins decorated in Lego prints or Paw Patrol.

Many families will already have an idea of what kind of day they wish for, including requesting the colour of clothes that attendees wear. They may have already discussed music, flowers and photographs they would like to use. Some may not have given it any thought at all. They may not even have had a chance to think about any of the things that could be considered.

When Dexter turned 1 month old, at the advice of the Sister at the hospital, we held a 1-month birthday party for him, as we knew he would never have his first birthday. He died 3 days later. As all our friends and family had met him and seen him on the day of his birthday, we opted for a private funeral. Honestly, I couldn't bear the pain of watching everyone I loved being so heartbroken for us, and we were in such a state of shock at everything that had happened, that it was exactly the right decision for us at the time.

Whichever way a parent decides to lay their child to rest is so personal and it is important to respect the decisions they make along the way.

Funerals for children in England are free, in that they are subsidised by the government. Some funeral homes may ask for payment upfront but that is not necessary, as they are able to claim the money back from the authorities. However, only the basics are covered. This includes the casket, service and burial or cremation. Things like flowers, carriages, horses, doves, and decorated caskets are available but do come at an extra cost.

WISDOM NUGGETS - THINGS YOU CAN DO IN THE FIRST WEEK

❖ Food and drink. The first few days are overwhelming and dark. Thinking about their own personal, human needs, may not be something parents can consider, so you can make sure they eat and stay hydrated as much as possible. Our bodies have a physical response to grief as well as a mental one, so it's important to try to keep parents' physical well-being in mind at this time. The cook at Derian House says that he is so grateful to have such a rewarding job. When he feeds a grieving family, he knows he is making a very real difference in how they will get through the coming days.

❖ Ask them, simply, what they need. Do they need to talk, cry, or sit silently? Tell them you are there; remind them they have space with you. Try to remember that it is ok for you to show your pain. Obviously, it is important to put the parents and siblings first, but being upset is natural and no one is asking you to "be strong."

❖ Allow parents to be however they want to be. There is no right or wrong in these moments, there is a great deal of shock, regardless of how expected or unexpected their child's death has been. Some parents may be visibly upset, some may appear numb. Everyone will respond differently and allowing them to have this space is paramount.

❖ If you feel you are able, you can offer to inform friends and acquaintances. Social media can be a truly wonderful tool, but it is important to say that sharing someone's death on social media before people have been personally informed can be incredibly distressing, so it should be avoided until its clear that the majority of family members and or close friends have been informed. You can ask the parents for a list of people they would like personally contacted, and when they would like it publicly announced. Not all parents will want people to know immediately. They will almost certainly be in a state of shock, and they may want time themselves to understand what has happened. Respecting this is paramount. Parents may also like to do announcements themselves, but you could offer to put together a reel of photographs or videos for them to use in their announcement. Again these are things parents may want to do themselves but it helps to know that someone else is there to ask.

❖ You can offer drive them to the Registry Office and have the money available for the death certificate, along with the correct paperwork such as the medical certificate. Registration is free but the certificate has a cost attached and parents must have this physical certificate in order to make funeral arrangements.

❖ You can call the **Tell Us Once** service on their behalf. You will need the information listed in the text box below but making this phone call can save the family distress in the coming weeks and months. This service didn't exist when Dexter died and the last thing I thought about was his Disability Living Allowance. I assumed when he died, it would stop. 6 months to the day of his death, I got a letter from the DLA people saying that we didn't inform them and we now owed them money! It wasn't about the money, it was the fact that in the most difficult moment of our lives we were supposed to have thought about calling a government department to tell them our son had died.

❖ For some parents, rooms of rest (Cold rooms) can become an anchor so it's important to try to help them take the steps gently back in to the world where you can. Taking them for a coffee, reminding them to eat, looking at photographs of their child together, these kinds of things can help them start to take the steps back in to the world.

❖ It can be helpful to have suggestions at hand for funerals/ celebrations of life. There will be lots of things that we may not have ever imagined could be done! Helping to do things like pull together video or photographs is a good idea, along with suggesting and coordinating things like music and decoration.

❖ You can help lo arrange pallbearers if needed. Speak with the funeral director regarding how many are needed, bearing in mind that a child's coffin is smaller and lighter so will probably not require as many people to carry it. Babies' coffins will often be carried by one or both of their parents, but it is different for everyone and of course, a very personal decision.

❖ There are so many wonderful ideas for things to do at funerals that truly celebrate the life of a beloved child. One particularly beautiful thing I've seen is the inclusion of a memorial tree in which people were asked to write a memory of the child or message on a small wooden heart and hang it on the tree. The family planted that tree in their garden and the messages are in a frame in their home. There are so many wonderful things that can be done on the day (or afterwards). Do some research and offer some options. (There is also a list of various websites listed in the back of this book).

❖ Many families will ask for donations to organizations that have assisted them. Communicating this and coordinating with said organizations can be something you can assist with if needed.

❖ There are many options now in terms of memorialising, including the donation of trees or plants, benches or jewellery made from ashes. Research the options for parents so that they know what is available. I remember saying to Chris on that first day that I wanted something that had Dexter's ashes in it. Back then there weren't a lot of options but we had a jeweller who very kindly worked with us to make me a ring with some of his ashes set in to it. Since then, there are some amazing companies that do all manner of things from jewellery to Christmas decorations.

❖ In every family's home it reflects the people who live there, including our child who has passed away. If you can, offering to help go through things that need sorting can be helpful, or even offering to be there after parents have done this can be incredibly important for moral support. Going through our childs things can be very distressing but also an important part of our grieving process so it should be encouraged but not expected. How parents will deal with this part will be as different as different can be. I've known people to get rid of everything, and I've known people who have taken years to even change elements of a bedroom. I found it helpful to give away things to people that I loved who were having babies. I felt like they knew that their gift of Dexter's things was made with thought and love and was reserved for people important to me. It felt like a gift from him. It will be a very individual decision though. Reminding your loved one that don't have to be alone in this part is very thoughtful.

❖ For children who had complex needs, there may well be equipment in the home that will need to be either collected by the Local Authority or can be donated to help another child with complex needs. Whilst I don't want to be critical of Local Authorities, they can have a reputation for being a little mercenary about collecting equipment once they have been informed of a child's death. Helping to prepare equipment to be collected can be helpful, as this may be a difficult task for parents at this time. For some parents, knowing that equipment is going to someone who needs it can be a great source of comfort, so you could research in your area, through your networks to find out if there are any children locally in need and suggest donation. This is something that will be a very individual decision, so please tread with care and try not to be too many steps ahead of parents at this point.

❖ I wish many, many times that someone had told me to take more time off. I once read of a woman who took to her bed for 6 months after her child died and I have been so jealous of that woman over the years! Whilst I don't think I needed 6 months of sleep, I definitely tried to get back to "real life" far too quickly. I was trying so hard to make everyone else feel better that I didn't take the time for myself. I am pragmatic so it felt right for me, but I had often thought that had I a mum like other women I know, she may have told me to slow down and take some time. Encourage loved ones to do things in their own time but also remind them that they are allowed to stop and do nothing loo. Many Limes, families will start charities or start fundraising, and whilst this is incredible and necessary, and can be a welcome distraction, sometimes it is ok to just not do anything.

❖ Many families will want to fundraise and as I say, this is incredible. You can help by researching and suggesting ways that parents can support charities in their child's name. It is important to say that whilst it is an amazing thing to start your own charity, it is a very, very difficult thing to do properly and involves a lot of work and bureaucracy, so if there is already a charity that does what parents want to do, it may sometimes be a better option to fundraise in their child's name for that existing charity. Again though, for some, a charity may be how they want to keep their child's name alive, so it is once again an important personal decision.

WHAT YOU NEED FOR THE TELL ME ONCE SERVICE

What you need when you call Tell Us Once:

- ❖ surname
- ❖ date the child died
- ❖ the name and address of their next of kin
- ❖ if they died in a hospital, nursing home, care home or hospice, the name and address of that institution - you'll also be asked if the stay was for 28 days or more

You may also need:

- ❖ if they had a passport, their passport number and town of birth
- ❖ if they owned any Motability vehicles, the vehicle registration number
- ❖ if they were getting services from their local council, the name of their local council and which services they were getting
- ❖ if they had a Blue Badge, their Blue Badge number
- ❖ if they were getting any benefits, such as Disiblity Living Allowance, information about which ones they were getting.
- ❖ If the child was over 16, you'll also need their National Insurance number.

THE FIRST YEAR.

Once we are through the most acute elements, no matter how it is being approached, we will have gone back to our homes and started to look at the world through a different lens.

We now have a greater understanding of the worst things a person can endure. Things that may have annoyed us in the past may glide off us easily. The everyday annoyance of traffic or parking seems insignificant compared to the pain we feel. I am absolutely someone now who is not phased by the *big things* so much anymore. If you crashed my car, I'd say, "Are you ok?" and we would take it from there. No big deal. That said, if I drop a fork whilst I'm cooking, you might want to leave the room as I will 100% lose it. I definitely sweat the small stuff!

To begin with, I felt like nothing would ever be fun again. As though there was no place for joy. It felt like sadness reigned and I was nothing but a lady in waiting, resigned to managing this palace of despair I was now a part of until my own life was done.

I think within a few months, whilst the hurt remained, the days got a little easier in that I was probably not as consumed by it. However, very quickly the next difficult part starts.

The firsts.

Birthdays, Christmas, Mother's and Father's Day. All these days and more can bring that more acute pain back to the surface and many times, those around us are not necessarily aware that these days can take us right back to where we were when our child initially died.

What many people won't realise is that there is another set of times that can also be really challenging. 6 months. I had no idea how much this point would affect me. It is this strange halfway milestone. The pain is no longer as visceral perhaps (for some), but it still feels so overwhelming, and yet, by this point, it can feel like the rest of the world has simply moved on. Everyone is back living their lives and we still wake every morning hoping the last months were nothing but a terrible nightmare.

I still had the *"Magic Moment"* every day at this point too. This is the moment when you wake but are not quite conscious yet. It is where you may begin to experience the feeling that everything is as it was before. Then you actually do wake up and reality sets back in.

It's no one's fault they don't see these timeframes as important, and people can't be expected to realise. For many of us, however, we see significance in dates that we would never have seen in any other situation. To begin with, we are taking one day at a time, then before we know it we are counting months and moving further away from when our child was once alive.

In the first year, most people do tend to be a little more aware those dates are coming, and we are often still at a point where we will be reminding people that a special day is on the horizon, so this first set is frequently marked by the people around us.

Doing things on these "firsts" are enormously appreciated gestures that will come to mean the world to parents.

For our first Christmas without Dexter, some of our friends bought a "star" for him and gave us the certificate. It was such a kind gesture and brought us to tears. We had it framed, along with one of our favourite photographs of him and it now hangs proudly in our home, alongside our many other pictures of his angelic little face.

Almost universally, bereaved parents agree that the lead-up to these significant days is actually worse than the days themselves.

I am hesitant to write this next part as it is not something I would normally say to anyone who is in the early throes of their loss, but I think it is important to understand.

Although the first year was utterly devastating, I never expected that the second year would feel so much harder. I am still not really sure why, but I think there was an expectation that it was a long enough time that

I should have been fine by then. Perhaps it was that I had gone head first into fundraising and trying to help other people, that I still hadn't really come to any kind of terms in my head about what had happened. I also had undiagnosed PTSD, so there were a whole lot of issues at play, not to mention the new, demanding baby I was trying to pour all my heart into.

WISDOM NUGGETS - THINGS YOU CAN DO IN THE FIRST YEAR

- ❖ Again, acknowledgement is key here. Recognising that these firsts for us will be difficult is paramount. Even though they may not hold value to anyone else, they can be visceral reminders of our loss.

- ❖ Significant days like Christmas are a good time for small gifts in memory of. My sister-in-law buys a decoration every year for Dexter and there is always a candle on our Christmas dinner table.

- ❖ Fundraising around a significant day is a wonderful way Lo pay Lribule and show parents you are thinking of them. Things like bike rides and fun runs are run by many and varied charities all across the UK.

- ❖ Hosting a small get-together for birthdays can be a lovely way to celebrate with parents.

- ❖ Random Acts of Kindness. Taking time to do something kind for a stranger, in a late child's name is a lovely gesture that has grown in popularity. Many families now have cards printed that they leave when they have done said act with their child's name.

- ❖ On Dexter's birthday, we leave money with the management at favorite eatery, for them Lo pay randomly for a family's bill. We ask the management Lo choose a family who have been polite and lovely and tell them that it has been paid for in memory of a little boy named Dexter. We choose to do this anonymously but that is a personal choice for us. (Although I am aware this is now not anonymous!)

❖ Arrange a candle lighting amongst other family and friends and send photos to parents to show them how many people are thinking of them.

❖ There are many gift ideas now for anniversaries, things like painted stones or ceramics with quotes available that can feel very special to receive.

❖ Most families will have a symbol or symbols they hold dear for their child. Dexter's symbol is a star so our home is constantly filled with stars regardless of what time of year it is. Both Chris and I have star tattoos in his memory. Mine is coloured in blue, like Dexter's eyes but Chris only has the outline as he watched me get mine and decided "for artistic reasons" he wanted it over and done with quickly!

❖ Every gesture doesn't need to be large. Sending a love heart or a "thinking of you" text are all great ways to let parents know you are thinking of them.

THE "AFTER".

Many of the things I have talked about so far are the things that you can help with in the very beginning of a family's bereavement, but it is important to point out that whilst this part of your help is greatly appreciated, where you can often make the most impact is further down the line.

Eventually, life calls people back and whilst we know you care about us, you go back to your normal lives, and we know that nothing in our lives will ever be "normal" again. Very quickly, it can feel like everyone has forgotten. This can feel like a whole new pain.

We are getting a lot better at allowing people to share their grief and thanks to the brave sharing of some people in the public eye. There are more and more platforms appearing with encouragement for bereaved parents to share their experiences and the memories of their children. Doing this online doesn't remove the need for real human interaction when bereaved. That is where we still desperately need you.

I will say this as diplomatically as I possibly can, not all online support is necessarily healthy for a bereaved parent. Forums and groups can be a wonderful place to get the support you need, especially if you are not blessed with supportive family and friends, but like any online interaction, we need to be careful not to cut ourselves off from those we love in the real world, even though we might not be ready to come back into that world just yet. We need to make sure that the groups we are in are right for us and the place we are in. Online friendships are still genuine friendships, that is very important to acknowledge. We learnt from Covid that personal contact holds a much more important place in our lives than we possibly realised before it was taken away from us for a while. This is why your support is so crucial. Sometimes we will need you to help guide us back to things, to hold our hands, literally and metaphorically, as we start to do things we did before our world fell apart.

Online groups and forums absolutely have an important role to play. They may help us to communicate our truest thoughts and feelings, as these are often with other members of *The Club*, so we can feel safety in them that we may not feel in the real world. Both virtually and physically, we need to know that there are people who will listen to why going back to things is so hard, why it hurts and why we want to talk about it. It is helpful if we can do that both online and in person.

There may be times, I am certain, that we frustrate you or even make you angry. Not all our behaviour will be rational or fair or reasonable, but I implore you to be patient. Understand that nothing is the same for us and for many people grief can make them make bad decisions. Behaviour that numbs the pain isn't unusual, and whilst this can be tough to witness, with gentle love and compassion, you can see us through to the other side.

Sometimes, sadly, grief can manifest in more complicated ways. Understanding what these look like can help you recognise if someone you love may be suffering in a way that seems different to what is conventionally expected.

This table outlines the different kinds of grief that someone may experience. These are not limited to child loss but may help give you some insight if someone you love appears to be struggling in a way you can't quite understand. It may also help you identify if your loved one appears to need some more specialised help.

DIFFERENT TYPES OF GRIEF

Normal grief

The American Psychology Association defines normal grief as grief that lasts 6 months to 2 years following the significant loss. There may be cultural differences to consider as well. For example, some cultures have grieving practices that call families together over a period of several years to mourn the deceased.

Absent grief

Absent grief is when there is a complete void of grief in response to a great loss. This is more common when the loss is sudden. You can recognize absent grief by the presence of denial and shock. Absent grief should be addressed if it continues for an extended period of time.

That said, it's important to remember that everyone's grieving process is slightly different. So if you suspect someone is struggling with absent grief, you should be cautious to address it. They could be showing their grief in a more subtle way but still experiencing extreme turmoil within.

Just because someone doesn't look like they're grieving, doesn't mean that they aren't. If you're experiencing this type of grief, you could be grieving but completely unaware of it. There's often a lot to manage around the time of loss, so you may not have the time or capacity for intense feelings right now. Or you may simply grieve more subtly, and that's okay.

Anticipatory grief

This type of grief is felt in anticipation of a significant loss. This includes things like the diagnosis of a terminal illness, anticipated layoffs, or impending divorce. It is common for caregivers to feel anticipatory grief over a terminally ill patient or loved one.

When experiencing anticipatory grief, you may start envision-
ing your life without that person. You might make plans for
what how you will respond to the loss, or want to prepare for
its occurrence.

Living in this anticipation can be challenging, however. You
may feel conflicted over the guilt of planning for a loved one's
departure. Or you might feel resolved in the peace you have
time to make prior to experiencing the loss. Either way, it is
important to be patient with yourself as you navigate this type
of grief.

Delayed grief

This grief reaction does not occur for a long time after the loss
occurred. Sometimes delayed grief surfaces in the face of another significant loss down the line. It functions like a trigger,
opening the gates from the initial loss.

DIFFERENT TYPES OF GRIEF

Complicated grief

This type of grief experience is marked by conflicting feelings for the loss. For example, grief over the death of an estranged parent or abusive partner, or the loss of a job that no longer brought joy.

Cumulative grief

Grief of this type builds up over time and is marked by a number of losses taking place in a relatively short period of time. The fatigue felt by many in the face of the COVID pandemic is a type of cumulative grief.

Disenfranchised grief

Kenneth Doka, Ph.D., writes in Disenfranchised Grief: Recognizing Hidden Sorrow, that this type of grief occurs anytime someone feels that society has denied their "need, right, role, or capacity to grieve." Examples of disenfranchised grief include hidden or secret relationships, pets, or where the loss is seen as small by others or minimized by the culture.

Distorted grief

Often characterized by an extreme reaction, distorted grief provokes an intense response from the griever. This type of grief can be identified by the griever's immense emotional response and often hostile behavior.

This anger is directed at other people and/or the griever themselves. Be aware of episodes of lashing out, and check in with the griever to ensure they aren't in a position to hurt themselves or another person.

Inhibited grief

This type of grief reaction occurs when someone does not show any type of outward grief. They often remain very busy or distracted. They could take on more work or start new projects to keep their minds occupied and avoid dealing with their grief.

This pattern continues for a long time. Often the individual usually develops a physical manifestation of their grief. This can be stomach issues, poor sleep, muscle and body aches, etc. The physical symptoms vary but are usually present with inhibited grief.

Abbreviated grief

Abbreviated grief passes quickly. This type of grief is short-lived as individuals move on quickly. They can feel the urge to find a substitute to fill the space the departed has left. Or they can already have made peace with their loss prior to it actually happening.

Chronic grief

If you still have very strong emotions around grief for months or years following the initial loss, you may be experiencing chronic grief. This differs from normal grief in that the feelings do not come and go. Nor do they lessen in intensity. With chronic grief, the griever has an incredibly difficult time dealing with their grief or overcoming it.

Collective grief

Some events cause entire communities and large groups of people to suffer. Events such as terrorist attacks, war, and pandemics are common causes of collective grief. There doesn't have to be a direct connection between the loss or tragedy and the community, however. The death of a public figure can also cause collective grief.

As I have mentioned several times, the real grief for us doesn't just lie in the physical death of our child. Our grief is the love that has nowhere to go. It's the moments we will never have, the laughter we will never share. There will be no birthdays, graduations or weddings. No first day of school, no last. As you read the list of what we miss, perhaps it is a little clearer why the lack of acknowledgement can make us feel isolated and angry.

Many of these things you take for granted when you decide to have a family. You enter into a virtual contract with life that you will watch this child grow into an adult. All from the moment you knew they would come barrelling into your life kicking and screaming and covered in some goop that somehow didn't make you gag when you saw them the first time. That squishy, beautiful new human being is your future. It is your gift to the world.

When they die, this is all gone.

As difficult as it is, getting into some sense of what is normal for us now is important and as we navigate our place in our new world, we are trying to discover what remains. Going out, meeting friends, working, hobbies. These are all things that we may come back to. For some, the focus may go entirely into charity work or raising awareness, and all of this is ok because part of our grieving is learning how we exist in the "real world" now that it is forever changed.

When a child dies, their parent has a profound need to try to keep their memory alive. It can feel like your number one priority. We will never be able to make any more memories with our children, so saying their name and sharing their lives, helps us to spend time with them once again, even if it is only in our minds. The world needs to know who they were because they were here and however long that may have been, they changed our lives forever. So now we need to make sure no one ever forgets. People will try. People will talk as though they never existed and all we want to do is tell you to *say their name!*

There is no reason for you to ever stop saying it. We need you to under-stand that we are trying to find a way to live without their name, and life, being a core part of our daily existence. We are trying to make sure the world doesn't forget they were here.

Time passes and somewhere along the way, our child's name is not said daily in the company of others, and eventually, as heartbreaking as it is when you realise, it is not even said from your own mouth day to day. Of course, the moment you have the thought that today you hadn't felt their loss enough, you laughed too hard, or you felt content for a moment, guilt sprints back in, ready to stand, winning, atop a podium of sorrow.

A shift happens in the way people look at you when you bring your child's name up after a while. We know their death makes you uncomfortable. It makes us pretty uncomfortable too, believe me. Earlier we explored the why, let's talk about the how.

Even now, when I mention Dexter, I feel the eye roll of some people. "Oh, this again. Why doesn't she just get over it? Why does she *always* have to talk about it??"

To those of you who do this, we see you. You may think we don't notice, but bereaved parents have a sixth sense for this stuff, and we know when you do it. Perhaps more importantly though, I hope you never have a real, proper understanding, because the only way to have that is to live through it, which I don't ever want for anyone. Those fears you have for your own children's safety; we know all too well the worst-case scenario. There but for the grace of God and all that.

Some people may even try to justify their lack of patience with our grieving by bringing up the fact that there are currently living children suffering in poverty or war and the like. Yes, that is also something we see. Despite my husband's insistence that I cannot multi-task, I can walk and chew gum at the same time. Just as I can love my surviving children and grieve daily for Dexter. I can obsessively binge watch "Married at First Sight Australia" and yet still believe it to be the worst television show I have ever seen.

People are capable of thinking of and caring for many things. Caring about keeping our children's memories alive, doesn't mean we don't care

[121]

about anything else, in fact, I often think it makes us care more. Only now we care with the experience of having had it all taken away.

Like our grief, all these things apply for the rest of our lives. All of the things I have said that are helpful will always be so, to some extent. Sure, some practical things won't apply, but I'd like to think by reading this far, you are now a bit of an expert in helping your loved one and advocating for them too. Even having done perhaps just one or two of the things I have suggested, I am sure you will have made an extraordinary impact.

It will often be the little things you do that are the most important. Drawing our child's symbol on a Christmas card or sending a picture of a lit candle on a significant day. These sorts of powerful, simple gestures will cement your place in our lives.

FINALLY

Life has a way of taking over and for many bereaved parents, we may well find that unless we do a lot of specific work in the world of child loss, we have moved through to a different, but often, good life, despite having had such a terrible thing happen. It is not to say we forget, but that we have, for want of a better word, accepted it as a part of who we are and that it shaped us into better humans. I am a far better person now because Dexter came into my life and took a piece of my heart.

I was so broken when he died, and somehow I knew that would be how I would remain for the rest of my days. Nothing would ever piece me together again. I didn't know if I would ever feel hopeful about anything in the future. I knew though, that I had to make his death mean something. I had to find some reason in it all, so I guess I always knew my life would end up dedicated to helping bereaved parents find ways to share their children with the world. I became an Ambassador for Derain House shortly after his death, and in 2018, in one of my proudest moments, they invited me to be their official Patron. This role has allowed me such a wonderful understanding of what they do to help so many people but has also shown me immense shortfalls around bereavement care in this country. My passion is creating platforms for these families and elevating their voices.

I also started The Keepsake Circle, alongside my dear friend Angus Powell, working with bereaved families, writing original songs in tribute to beautiful children, gone too soon. Music gives these families a wonderful platform to share their children with the world, for ever more.

Something wonderful happened when I started working with other bereaved parents. I have yet to meet a more hopeful human than a parent who has buried their child. They seem to have a way of seeing the world through a shattered, but somehow kinder, lens. They allow me the privilege of listening to the stories of their children, and how their worlds were changed because of a special child who was not long for this world.

So now, in the quiet moments, I feel all their names etched upon my heart, next to Dexter, never to be forgotten. Their light may have faded too soon, but it is an eternal flame within me that drives me to make the world a better place for their parents. Whilst I live and breathe, I will shine their light.

And as for Dexter, as long as we are living, our baby you will be.

Love, Mummy.

RESOURCES

WONDERFUL ORGANISATIONS
I HAVE MENTIONED.

I couldn't possibly list all of the incredible organisations out there that are available for support, but it is important that I include some of the magical places that have made my journey to this point possible.

www.derianhouse.co.uk

www.togetherforshortlives.org.uk

wwww.reubensretreat.org

www.maggiesstillbirthlegacy.org.uk

www.jordansretreat.org.uk

www.remembermybaby.org.uk

https://www.sands.org.uk

https://www.tommys.org

ORGANISATIONS THAT OFFER SUPPORT AFTER THE DEATH OF A CHILD.

This is a snapshot of some of the UK organisations that offer support to families after the death of a child. There are more focused support networks based on conditions and illnesses but I have decided to leave this a bit more general. There are links to all of these organisations and more on my website.

www.childbereavementuk.org

www.thegoodgrieftrust.org

www.sands.org.uk

www.tommys.org

www.tcf.org.uk

www.cruse.org.uk

www.lullabytrust.org.uk/bereavement-support

www.sayinggoodbye.org

SUPPORT FOR BEREAVEMENT
FOR SUDDEN DEATH.

Accidents and accidental death are also an area that may require more specific support and these are some of the valued UK support organisations available.

www.rvtrust.org.uk

www.rlss.org.uk/listing/category/support-for-families

www.tcf.org.uk/ftb-road-traffic-incident

www.brake.org.uk

SUPPORT FOR BEREAVEMENT
FROM SUICIDE.

As discussed, different types of death can require different types of support, and suicide is one of these. Again, this is not an exhaustive list but some of the UK organisations that specialise in this area.

www.suicideandco.org

www.winstonswish.org

www.ifucareshare.co.uk

www.papyrus-uk.org/suicide-bereavement-support/

Giving a voice to the child left behind. Maddie Roberts. Published 2024. (A publication for supporting children after suicide).

RITUALS WITHIN OTHER RELIGIONS AND CULTURES

As I am no theological expert, I have drawn some information online that I felt was easy to access and offered valuable insights on how other cultures ritualise death.

Overview

www.pdscp.co.uk/wp-content/uploads/2019/09/110.-Cultural-Awareness-for-when-a-Child-dies.pdf

Judaism

mourning/

www.funeralpartners.co.uk/help-advice/arranging-a-funeral/types-of-funerals/jewish-funeral-customs/

Islam

www.jewishmuseum.org.uk/schools/asset/life-cycle-death-www.artofdyingwell.org/caring-for-the-dying/deathbed-etiquette/islamic-rituals/www.childbereavementuk.org/FAQs/islam

Hinduism

www.childbereavementuk.org/FAQs/hinduism

Buddhism

www.childbereavementuk.org/FAQs/buddhism

Chinese communities

www.childbereavementuk.org/FAQs/chinese-communities

www.mariecurie.org.uk/talkabout/articles/chinese-death-traditions/358268

MEMORIALISING

There are just some ideas for memorialising. There is an enormous amount of ways to choose from now, but these are some of my favorite places that do this, along with a guide for things you can do. This is not an exhaustive list.

Overview

www.tcf.org.uk/resources/Remembering- Our-Child-Handbook.pdf

Trees & Plants

www.thepresenttree.com/collections/memorial-trees

www.woodlandtrust.org.uk/blog/2024/02/dedicate-trees-in-memory/

Jewellery

www.silverdovememorialjewellery.co.uk

www.everwith.co.uk

www.handonheartjewellery.co.uk/collections/memorial-bereavement-jewellery

Memory bears & textiles

www.memorybears.co.uk

infinitykeepsakegifts.co.uk/product-category/clothing-keepsakes/memory-bears/

Keepsakes

www.thelovelykeepsakecompany.co.uk/collections/bereavement-gifts

www.etsy.com/uk (Etsy have a huge selection of keepsake options).

GUIDED MEDITATIONS

Here are some wonderful sites that use guided meditation to help with grief.

https://www.mindful.org/a-10-minute-guided-meditation-for-working-with-grief/

https://grateful.org/resource/a-meditation-on-grief/

https://griefhaven.org/meditations-for-grievers/

YouTube is a great resource for guided meditation.

ACKNOWLEDGEMENTS

My family. Private people who never asked to be a part of the public eye but have never done anything but support my career, and most importantly, this book. I thank you all from the bottom of my heart. L&P, CMLO, M&M, Alec, Paris & Pheonix.

Ribqah, Reuben and Maggie, and importantly, your mamas; Samailah, Nicola and Sarah.

Being able to tell the stories of these three incredible children has been an honour and a privilege. I am so grateful that you are all in my life, and I am especially grateful that I could have a small part in making sure that all your names are heard and honoured by hopefully at least, a few more people. Thank you for trusting me and thank you for always being there and reminding me that we truly all can make a difference.

My dear friend and Author, Heidi Mavir who always told me I needed to write a book and then finally kicked me up the butt (with love) to do it! I do love you so.

Abi and Lisa at the team at Authors and Co, who gave me the most incredible knowledge which meant I could put all this into words. You are opening doors for so many people, and that is magical. Thank you so, so much. As an extension of this team, Maddie Roberts, who has supported me and given so much encouragement.

Sarah Mills. You reminded me to bring myself into the writing. You are funny and kind and honest and remind me why humour is so important. Thank you for your incredible guidance and insight, and for the occasional gag.

Dr Laurie Powell. Godmother extraordinaire and palliative consultant. I feel like those that you treat are so fortunate to have a doctor with so much compassion and love. You knew right from the start that I adore what medicine and its practitioners are capable of, and you helped so much in making sure that I got this across. You will always remain younger than me, and for that, I will always resent you a bit. I love you and thank you.

Caroline Taylor. Working with you at Derian House has been such a pleasure for me, and every time I see you I feel like you are always working towards making sure the world as a whole is a better place. Thank you for your wonderful guidance, and corrections when needed.

Helen Fogg. Getting to know you and see how you help families is incredible and I am so lucky that I have benefitted from your experience and knowledge. I know that if you are helping a bereaved family, they are getting the very best help available.

Lee Dancy. A girl couldn't find a more loyal and dynamic friend in you. You inspire me daily to be the best version I can be and to always have a plan. I am so grateful for your mentoring and guidance in not only this book but also in my other work. Thank you.

Kirsty Harris. Even though you knew this would be a tough read, you offered so very much to the process that I can't thank you enough for. Whilst I wish our paths hadn't crossed this way, I am so grateful to call you my friend now. Thank you to you and thank you to Iris for bringing us together.

Nicky, for always being one I could call on who would get it so much more than anyone else. L, you inspire me daily too, just like your Mama does.

Rebecca, Ang, Racheal, Flip, Tildie, Paula, Livia, Ionica, Emma, Gemma M, Bethany. Thank you for being my biggest cheerleaders. I love you all dearly.

Shelley, Nina and Gemma, thank you for helping, years of friendship and loyalty. I love you all dearly.

Gordon and Carolin. For decades of friendship, belief and teaching me how to adult. I love you both so very much. You are my family too.

Angus, as always, you inspire me daily and I am so grateful that because of you, I get to help create more platforms for families to share their children's stories. Here's to many more songs.

To every bereaved parent of every child I have had the privilege to hear about, I am so grateful that you have trusted me to hear your memories, your pain and your joy.

ABOUT THE AUTHOR

Kiki Deville is an award-winning entertainer from the "Lake District" of South Australia, Mount Gambier. A professional singer of over 35 years, she has appeared as a finalist on The Voice UK as part of Team Will-I-Am, along with several other TV credits to her name.

For 15 years, Kiki has been a sought-after and beloved host of Burlesque and Cabaret throughout the UK and Europe, headlining almost every major festival in the genre.

During the pandemic, without the ability to tour as normal, along with colleague Angus Powell, Kiki started the bespoke songwriting company The Keepsake Circle. Working through children's hospices across the UK, The Keepsake Circle meet with bereaved families, hear their stories and then write an original song in tribute the child who has died. So far, since 2022, they have released 4 albums.

With a passion for empowering voices, Kiki has spent the last 17 years trying to elevate the voices of bereaved parents and change the narrative around child loss.

Photograph by Terry Mac Photography Manchester

Printed in Dunstable, United Kingdom